A Tale
of
Two Iditarods

C. Mark Chapoton

Cover Art by Michael Chapoton.

Front cover photo of Martin Buser's 2007 Goose Bay 120 team by Kathy Chapoton.

Back cover based on a map created by Ray Sterner of The Johns Hopkins University Applied Physics Laboratory, licensed to North Star Science and Technology, LLC. Race route by author.

ISBN 978-0-6152-0652-3

Paperback Edition
Published by CMC
PO Box 520063
Big Lake, AK   99652

Available at Lulu.com

Copyright © 2008 Charles Mark Chapoton

Continuing dog mushing as a hobby.
photo: Nancy Stark

Skijoring in 2008 with Lynda Plettner's racing sled dogs.
photo: Trish Kolegar

ACKNOWLEDGMENTS

Nobody makes a real book alone. I am indebted to many people for both the experiences described in this work, and the preparation of this book. In no particular order, I acknowledge help of those named below.

Giant thanks are due to my Mom. Her love, compassion, and warm empathy combined to make me into a person who connects with animals. A great many of the recreational and aspiring mushers I meet treat the dogs as largely inanimate objects. To this unfortunate mass of people, the sled dogs are parts of the machine. Important parts, as worthy of care and attention as the NASCAR racer's car parts, but inanimate pieces in a machine built to get them and their egos quickly from here to there. For Martin, and the other ultra-competitive mushers, and me (though I am certainly not in their category vis-à-vis competitiveness or skill), the dogs are our friends, our helpers, and our dependents. Mom helped to raise me into someone who truly *likes* animals, and likes to be friends with them. The dogs had more fun, and I did better by them, because of that. That's a good thing.

I am indebted to my Father, without whom this book would not have been created. The notion to compile these two stories as this book was his. He also did the work transforming the ancient printed pages to electronic form, organizing, suggesting useful additions and adjustments, keeping track of the various iterations, minimally editing my unusual grammar, working the formatting, and the like. His name also goes on this list for encouraging my move from dismal circumstances in Texas to Alaska back in '91.

A redoubled thank you goes to the giant group of supporters and friends who helped me do these runs. Some of these fine folks are mentioned by name. All of them are remembered with a big smile. For different reasons, and at different times; nobody does the Iditarod alone.

Uncle Martin and Aunt Kathy, who, if listed in importance to this effort would surely get top billing, are due special thanks. In 1991 they opened their home to me when I moved to Alaska, and put up with my various foolishnesses. They allowed me to run in the Iditarod not once, but twice, with Martin's racing dogs. Sled dog racing is what he does for a living, and I am very grateful they made me a part of that. Dogsledding and skijoring are hobbies I continue to this day.

With Mom at Iditarod Sign-Up.
photo: Unknown

DISCLAIMER

These stories describe the events as I remembered them. As is well known, eyewitness' accounts recalled days, weeks, or months after an event are notoriously unreliable. I make no claim that what I have written represent the real reality of the events. Other participants undoubtedly have different recollections of the same events. Not everything described may seem exactly right to those who know better. And if some of my words seem to cast some characters sometimes in a negative light, that characterization is not an intentional slight. It's just how I remembered things.

Official Iditarod Finisher's Patch

PREFACE

I ran the Iditarod twice. I worked as a handler and trainer at Martin Buser's Happy Trails Kennel in Big Lake, Alaska. As part of the job I ran the yearlings in the Iditarod to test and train them. Martin won the race in 1992, the year before my first race, and again in 1994, my second year. He also won in 1997 and 2002. He and his dogs are among the few four-time winners. He is the unequaled four-time winner of the Leonhard Seppala Humanitarian Trophy which is the next best thing to winning the race. That award is given to the competitive musher who demonstrates outstanding and superior dog care throughout the race, and is voted by the official Iditarod veterinarian corps. I was working with the best of the best, my uncle.

I started writing these stories intending to include only the highlights of the race. Over the months after each race that I spent writing, though, it turned into something of a blow-by-blow account. Still, even at that, I don't lay out all my experiences. Some I can't write about with words, some are too personal, some were forgotten, and some times are just left out. I imagine that native story-tellers could take as many days as the musher took to complete the race, and communicate the entire essence of someone's Iditarod experience. These narratives are not that entire. Regardless though, they should bring the flavor across pretty well.

I recall the races as being very tough. When the going was good it was great, but there was a lot else in-between the good. Charles Dickens' *A Tale of Two Cities* begins: "It was the best of times, it was the worst of times…" That's an exactly spot on description of my Iditarod adventures. There were hours and hours of pure enjoyment and satisfaction. Sublime moments that defy the written word. Dogs' bootied feet in beautiful, colorful sync… mountains disappearing in the horizon… Northern Lights crackling green and red through glossy black nights… mushing at what seemed the top of the world. I try, but the million moments like that are hard to describe. There were also hours and hours of terrible effort and frustration. Small mistakes snowball on the Iditarod and become enormously difficult problems to overcome. An example of this was when my drag ripped off several times on exposed frozen stumps and rocks. The last time that happened, I refused to tie the team down and go back and get it again. That was coming down the Alaska Range foothills. No snow, just frozen ground. The brake was of less than no effect, and without question that drag would have made a big difference. We went too fast, and controlling the sled was backbreaking work and not entirely successful. I really wished I had that drag.

Running the Iditarod really can change you, like people often say, but not like they think. I used to say it didn't. Now I'm older and have a little more hindsight. Running the Iditarod forces you to find hidden parts of yourself, to look in your personal mirror, over and over. As you confront the extremes of the natural world on Iditarod, you experience the extremes of the inner self. Coming face to face with those aspects that the Iditarod mirror shows, can change who we act. Exactly how, who knows? Certainly, nobody asking the questions knows. Exactly how depends on so many things that a precise description defies the English language. An event so extraordinary that brings out so much extraordinary in us… it must change us somehow from who we were.

Iditarods XXI and XXII were far, far harder things than I'd ever done before.

I'd do it again with the right conditions, but one dog and one horse constitute what "kennel" I have now, and that is hardly appropriate for the 1,049 mile trek to Nome.

C. Mark Chapoton

Houston, Alaska

August 10, 2008

Solo the pet in lead with a team of rowdy puppies.
photo: Author

CONTENTS

PRELIMINARIES 1

IDITAROD XXI 15
    THE BEGINNING 17
        Finger Lake 23
        Rohn 26
    THE MIDDLE 33
        Iditarod 35
        Kaltag 38
    THE END 41
        White Mountain 46
        Nome 49

IDITAROD XXII 55
    THE BEGINNING 57
        Finger Lake 62
        Rohn 72
    THE MIDDLE 78
        Cripple 82
        Kaltag 88
    THE END 92
        White Mountain 98
        Nome 102

EPILOGUE 107

With members of the Pit Crew before the start. No Iditarod effort can be made without a lot of help. Many folks helped me. These are just a few of them.
photo: Unknown

PRELIMINARIES

The Iditarod Trail Sled Dog Race is a roughly twelve-hundred mile race across Alaska from Anchorage on the Pacific Ocean coast to Nome on the Bearing Sea coast. It starts the first Saturday in March; rain, snow, or shine. Each racing team consists of one human (the 'musher') and, when I ran the race, ten to twenty dogs. Sixty to eighty teams start. Forty to sixty teams finish. The race crosses the Alaska Range, home of Denali, the highest peak in the U.S., and runs two-hundred-odd miles on the mighty Yukon River. Alaska has just over half a million people in a state over twice the size of Texas. The race is through essentially uninhabited and unmolested terrain. Before the race, supplies (food and equipment) are cached at twenty-some remote checkpoints along the trail where veterinarians are on hand to assess and minister to the dogs' health. Dogs not at their best are "dropped" at checkpoints and flown back to Anchorage. Aside from the vets, no one is allowed to help the mushers during the race. Weather runs from a mild twenty above to fifty below with howling winds. Sometimes there is a lot of snow, sometimes there is very little, sometimes there is both, sometimes it rains. Storms frequently cover the trail with fresh deep drifts. The race is conducted by the Iditarod Trail Committee (ITC), with its headquarters in Wasilla.

THE RACE

The Iditarod Trail Sled Dog Race is a race between a musher and his dogs, and other mushers (men and women) and their dogs. Nowadays, the Iditarod is a fairly formal affair, with a thick rule-book to protect the dogs and keep things fair. Some of these rules are flexible. For example, no outside help, but, a musher can borrow a sled from a competitor to replace his shattered one, maybe even get one shipped in from a friend. Rules having to do with dog care are inflexible, for example: no dog abuse, no dog performance enhancing drugs, and the veterinarians have the final say anywhere anytime as to can a dog continue. Much of the rest of the rule book tries to keep things competitive. Outside help that gives a musher a competitive advantage is a big taboo. No laptop laden satellite dish support spy, no friends creeping out to do our chores… stuff like that. Like most Iditarod rules that have to do with the competition, the particulars of the "no outside help" rule have changed over the years after somebody goes past the intent and employs a unique scheme to get ahead. Most of these rules have somebody's name attached to them, informally of course. Once you get through all the rules, meetings, and ceremony, Iditarod is a break from everyday reality that is really a good thing to get to do.

The ITC recruits and manages an army (and Air Force) of volunteers to keep things on track. The Race Volunteers (almost everybody supporting the race as it happens) work long and hard to make the Iditarod a success every year.

Iditarod alternates between a Northern Route on even numbered years and a Southern Route on odd numbered years. This arrangement lets more interior villages play a part. Both routes spend time on the Yukon River, meeting at Kaltag; one going upstream against the wind, and the other going downstream against the wind. (It seems that on the Yukon, the wind is *always* in your face.) I liked the Northern Route better. The Northern split from Ophir to Ruby is much nicer to mush than Ophir to Shageluk, I thought.

Dogs are the priority. Always. More creature comfort is devoted to the dogs, by far, than for the mushers. Dogs that are taken out of a musher's team for lameness, tiredness, not eating, not drinking, sickness, slowness, or whatever, are held at checkpoints and flown back to the "HQ Hotel" in Anchorage for a quick stay and further vet evaluation before traveling to the local prison. There the inmates (those whose good behavior has warranted it) lavish care and attention on those early race retirees until the musher's rep comes to take them home.

Mushers don't have it too bad for most of the Iditarod, but accommodations change throughout the race, whereas for the dogs it is first class everywhere, every time.

THE DOGS

I must emphasize the unbelievable, incredible stamina and drive of the dogs. Folks who know the Iditarod consider the Alaskan Husky the premier athlete on the planet. They are bred to be intelligent and obedient, with a craving to run fast and long. They happily run ten hours or more a day, day after day on Iditarod, all the time pulling the musher and his gear. The musher who won the 2007 Iditarod also won the 2007 Yukon Quest, another thousand mile race (arguably tougher than the Iditarod). Just eleven days after winning the Quest, thirteen of his dogs that ran the Quest also ran in his winning Iditarod team. He got the cash and the new truck, but the dogs made it happen, and everyone who follows the Iditarod knows it. The ultra competitive musher takes all of his waking time on the trail, which is the vast majority of his time since sleep is a rare luxury, working to keep his dogs in top spirits and optimum health.

The Alaskan Husky is not an AKC-recognized breed, but a specialized dog bred to race in Alaska in the winter. They are smaller than most people think, averaging around fifty pounds. When they stand on four legs, most of them come up to my knee at the top of their shoulder. When most people think of a Husky, they think of something that looks like an Alaskan Malamute; a big, heavy, powerful, furry dog. The Alaskan Husky is very different. In appearance, the two differ like a rugby player differs from a marathoner. Ours have a deep chest, strong limbs and feet, a high, narrow waist, and a straight back. They have a two-layer short-hair coat to keep them warm and dry. Beyond basic build, no two look alike. It is a distinguishing characteristic of the breed to have random colors. Their conformation, or how they are put together and angulated, dictates a lot how they run. Really good bodies can effortlessly eat up the miles in a flat, smooth gait, pulling all the while.

As for temperament, while they are of course individuals, they seem to have two modes – one for relaxing, and one for running. On the chain at the kennel, they are friendly and playful. We encourage these natural tendencies through constant attention to socializing them to really like people. When the gangline comes out and we start to hook them up they get really keyed up. They lunge forward in harness, bark for all they're worth, and paw at the ground. The calm animal lounging on his house is transformed into a wild-eyed, spit-flying, straining-to-go maniac.

I call them "My Dogs" throughout these stories. Actually of course, they were Martin Buser's dogs. He selected the breeding, he planned the training, and he paid the bills. When I say "My Team", I mean the dogs I ran and became special friends with. Martin's dogs, though.

THE SLED AND RIG

Like a boat, there is a lot of equipment that goes into getting a quality dog sled to go just right. The first sled I built was old school, copied from one of Martin's favorites. It is all hickory, sandwiched plastic, bolts, string, varnish, and tough. The sled Martin built for me to use on the Iditarod was all hickory too, but a toboggan: a plastic bed just on top of the runners. Those are old school. New school is like modern jets; composites, aluminum, and wire cable.

The dogs are hooked to the sled by the gangline. Ganglines are sections of synthetic braided rope, eight feet or so long. They have steel cable in them. Tuglines, smaller than ganglines, attach the back of the dogs' harnesses to the gangline. The tuglines provide the pulling power. None of the lines have knots, they are all 'fidded' with eye splices and brass snaps that connect the lines to the dogs' harnesses.

Necklines attach the dogs' collars to the gangline. They don't pull with the necklines, instead, the necklines keep the dogs close to the gangline. Smaller snaps are used there so if a dog goes around the wrong side of a tree, the snap breaks and lets him be pulled around. When I ran, I figured I had a hundred feet of dogs. It was great.

Harnesses come in all sorts of shapes. Some pull off the middle of the back. Old school is to pull from the tail end. Some fit tight around the neck and shoulders, some rest just on the shoulders. They are all padded and reflective these days. I used new, top of the line stuff. Whatever Martin was using.

The sled has several things to slow it, stop it, and hold it stopped. There is a pronged foot brake that digs into the snow when it is pushed down. A piece of snowmachine track, the drag, is a speed control device. It hangs from the sled between the runners, and the musher puts weight on it for added resistance and a slower go. A snow hook (anchor) that the musher digs into the snow is connected right to the gangline by a rope long enough to be handy to the musher on the runners. The musher can slow the team with a heel on the drag, and stop the team with weight on the brake and/or by setting the snow hook. The sled can be anchored with a snow hook, or maybe two. Snow hooks can be heavy and big, but new school is light and specially shaped. Most mushers also have a quick release snap rope affair to tie up to trees with. All the lines, plus the sled, are connected to the gangline with the musher's favorite carabiner.

TRAINING

The Iditarod part of my job was to take the yearlings to Nome, NOT to race competitively. My goal was to finish with as many healthy dogs as possible. Martin takes adults to Nome with the goal of winning; getting there faster than anybody else. In the fall, Martin and I trained together, pairing yearlings with adults in the team. It was gritty and wet; the start of the training season coincides with the rainy season after the summer up here. It was a lot of fun though. The dogs became individuals and friends. Some boisterous, some shy, some serious, and some goofy. Every night the last chore I did was to go around and play with each dog in the yard, especially the ones I'd run, and the boss's money makers. That's how any handler's good day should end.

The yearlings learn from the adults how to run and pull. This is the case with most of their learning. We, the two-legs, don't teach them, the four-legs, much. They learn from the other dogs around them. So, during the early training season my dogs learned the basics – PULL. The brighter ones picked up on the fact that when the two-legs says something, the team is supposed to do something different. These become leaders. In 1993, these were Tatters, Christie, and Dingo.

They pull a 500-pound ATV around in the summer. This builds strength and muscle to protect their joints. When the snow is such that we can no longer use the 4-wheeler, we switch to sleds. Martin drove the adults, I ran the yearlings. We trained every day, rotating the dogs in and out of the team so each dog ran two days in a row, then got one day off. Martin went longer and longer, and did it quicker and quicker. I didn't go much further than thirty five miles, and held the dogs back all the way. The yearlings don't yet have the muscle mass to keep everything together should they be driven like competitive adults. So I went slowly. Turns out I might have gone too slowly. Most of my dogs got sold. (I now mush racing dogs, young and old, recreationally at a different pace; we fly. Martin's racing teams REALLY fly.)

They need to keep just having fun in harness. They'll be pushed enough later on when the boss is training to race, and they really need to have a love for pulling the sled as part of a team when it starts being work.

They run over a hundred miles a week, week in, week out, and they love it. When they are training, they don't seem to tire. When things are going best, they get stronger and faster the further we get into a run. They did, however, learn to flop down and start resting right quick on the Knik 200 (my Iditarod-qualifying race). All I had to do was feed them, keep them hydrated, tend to cut feet, and direct the show. The dogs do ninety percent of the work (the ten percent I do taking care of the pups and driving the sled, though, is some pretty hard work too).

That's the basic training. For the advanced course we (me and the dogs) camped out a lot, since we would be running for more than a few hours when we do the Iditarod. It helps to learn how to operate the equipment, and get a routine down for caring for the dogs away from the kennel. The dogs learn to be OK stopping, eating, and sleeping away from the familiar kennel. That held a special appeal for me as it meant I could sleep in, get home late, and the chores would be already done.

FOOD AND EQUIPMENT

What did I take along on the race? I took mandatory gear, additional essential gear, and food. There is not much room in the sled bag, so I was happy to learn on my camping trips what I could do without. A musher needs his axe, snowshoes, cooker, and sleeping bag. These items, also booties, dog food, and ITC promotional material, and the Vet Book, comprise the mandatory gear that the race checkers will look for. If you don't have it when you get to a checkpoint, you have to go back and find it. Essential gear takes up what little room is left in the bag. I need one small and two large coolers for personal and dog food respectively. A good bow saw is handy, as is a spare set of plastic runners. Wooden trail lath stakes come in handy to keep the cooker from melting into the snow and spilling. A small repair kit, a spare set of boot liners, and a large caliber pistol for moose are just about all I need.

I didn't take extra clothes, except for polypropylene underwear, socks, and lots of polypro and regular gloves. The Northern Outfitters suit I had was all I needed for any weather. Northern Outfitters, one of Martin's sponsors, provided us with super gear. One suit, one layer, got me through the whole race. It looks like a big black space suit.

The twenty-five hundred pounds of supplies that I shipped out to be cached at the checkpoints was 90% dog food. High grade commercial kibble (Eagle Pack Premium Pet Foods brand, another one of Martin's long time and highly valued sponsors) and beef is the standard meal. We supplement this with lamb, beaver, liver, tripe and fat sausage. The dogs tend to get finicky as the hard days go by, and we need to be able to present them with a variety of foods and soups to keep them eating. Dogs not eating, and more importantly not drinking, is a major problem for mushers on any distance race.

I had a variety of my meals vacuum packed and ready to go into the cooker hot water to heat up to fuel myself. My board of fare included shrimp and pasta sautéed in garlic and butter sauce, beef Stroganoff, macaroni and cheese and meat, grilled cheese sandwiches, flank steak, Little Caesar's (then one of Martin's sponsors) pizza, sausage McMuffins, poptarts, cake, candy, cookie dough, and a full McDonald's meal for the half-way point and Unalakleet (the first checkpoint on the Bearing Sea coast). I drank Capri-Sun foil packed juice drinks. The same principle regarding dog appetites applies to the musher, so I had a wide variety.

At each checkpoint, I loaded up from my cached supplies with enough food, booties, etc., to get me to the next, plus some extra, and shipped used but still usable stuff home. I usually camped twice for five or six hours between checkpoints.

One other thing of note. I carried an Argus global satellite tracking device. A grade-school class lesson package, part of the Great Alaskan Teaching Adventure, was being taught about the Iditarod by interested school teachers across the U.S. As part of the course, students could track two mushers who carried the "bricks". I was one. (Martin would have carried it, but the device is too heavy: three pounds of non-essential weight is too much for a serious competitor to carry.) The Argus had the capability to transmit a few standard messages, like "I'm Hurt", or "I'm Lost", or "Send Help". These capabilities were exercised both years I carried it, although not as intended.

SuperChamp Martin Buser with several racing sleds. Martin is a four time Iditarod champion and four time recipient of the Leonhard Seppala award for top dog care by a competitive musher. He owns and operates Happy Trails Kennel, where I did my thing.
photo: Author

Brushing dogs; important for bonding as well as maintaining the racers in top condition.
photo: Martin Buser

Repairing dog houses is a constant chore. It was a lot of fun. I had an audience, a show, and some good man-work.
photo: Kathy Chapoton

Puppies in a feeding frenzy over their dinner. Children visiting in the pupppy pens are often surprised by the similar exuberance of the older pup's greetings. I call it the shark pen.
photo: Kathy Chapoton

IDITAROD XXI

Writing about it after the race, it is almost like a dream. During the Iditarod, it got to seeming like that was my whole life. Travel... Take care of the dogs... Eat... Sleep... Feed the dogs... Eat... Pack the sled... Hook up the team... Travel... Stop... Check in... Take care of the dogs... Medicate the feet... Eat... Sleep... Feed the dogs... Pack up... It seemed like that is all I had ever done in my life, and all I was ever going to do. Go forward... Stop... Check in... Do the dogs... Eat... Sleep... Do it again... It was a great time. For over two weeks I had no home, and no responsibilities, but my sled and team. I always had family and friends, I knew they were behind me, but for two weeks, I was alone with my dog team traveling across Alaska – over much of the hardest-to-traverse trail (excepting perhaps the Yukon Quest race trail) on the continent. It is still strange to think about it. I went across the top of the world, through an ice hole into the river at the bottom of the Dalzell Gorge, and so far down the trail that whole mountain ranges sank into the horizon behind me. I went through a pretty severe storm on the coast so surreally beautiful that I forgot to be afraid for hours at a time.

I ran, sweated, cursed, hallucinated, and slept awake, was ecstatic, was angry, was amazed, and was stunned by the beauty. I worked 'til I trembled, and struggled 'til I screamed, and went on. Months after it was over, I couldn't wait to do it again.

I knew long before I started that I could not imagine what the Iditarod would be like. I had no frame of reference. Nobody could have made me believe and understand what a person goes through on the Iditarod trail.

With cousins Rohn and Nikolai Buser, before the start.
photo: Kathy Chapoton

THE BEGINNING

The Start in Anchorage, March 6, 1993, went flawlessly. I had a great crew who took care of my every need. They fed me and my dogs and scooped the poop. I had about a dozen friends, friends of friends, and friends of the family helping to keep my situation under control.

When it was time to move up to the starting line, another dozen or so Eagle Pack people were on hand to help guide the team up the chute. Almost all the other mushers had handlers hold on to the dogs' lines and pull them back. People were stepping on dogs' feet and stumbling all around. When I saw Martin go up, his handlers jogged forward in two parallel lines on either side of the team. Instead of having people hold the dogs back, he had a crew of big guys holding the sleds back.

We did the same thing. It looked pretty slick. The dogs ran slowly, and in a controlled fashion, by themselves up the starting chute with a line of blue jacketed men and women jogging along each side.

While the starter was counting down from twenty seconds, a TV news reporter decided it was a good time to stick his microphone in my face. I saw him coming and couldn't believe he wanted to interview me counting down in the Iditarod starting chute. He asked me how I was feeling and I told him I was REALLY nervous. The Marshall got to fifteen seconds to go, and the reporter asked me what I was thinking. A lot of responses went through my mind, most of them pretty profane, but I told him that I was through talking. I had an Iditarod to start.

I wasn't lying to that reporter either, I was REALLY nervous. I've been to court, to finals, graduate school orals and comps, and waited for 'The Word' many times. During my first Iditarod start, I was more nervous, anxious, stomach tied, and uptight than I had ever been in my life.

Then the starter said "Go!!," and all of a sudden, we were alone. I had my second sled rider of course, but the crowds were behind us, and the Iditarod trail was under the runners.

The dogs performed flawlessly during the run through the city. The spectators, cars, pedestrian bridges and tunnels didn't faze them at all. I imagine the entrances to tunnels under the road and the bridges over the highways have balled up more than a few dog teams on their run out of Anchorage. It is a credit to the breeding and training here at Happy Trails that my young dogs performed so well. They were incredibly stressed; surrounded by noise, and confronted with totally novel, and potentially threatening stimuli, and never balked once. I was happy enough, and we had a fine run to Eagle River followed by an uneventful trucking to the Wasilla restart, and another flawless run through Knik, and on to Flat Horn Lake, our first camp.

When we got to Flat Horn Lake, I parked the team at the end of a line of resting teams with my leaders on the bank. I secured the dogs, or so I thought, did the checkpoint routine, and went to sleep on top of my sled. I had planned to sleep 'til five in the morning (three hours or so) but did not wake to my alarm and slept 'til seven thirty.

It wasn't the sun coming up either that woke me. My leaders, Tatters being the chief culprit, had chewed the line that connected the front of the gangline to the front snow hook. The team was in a big ball back by the sled, and my pups had bumped me awake tangling themselves on top of me. My young leader, Tatters, was busy practicing making babies with little brown Christie, who I had put way back in wheel just because she was in heat. Smart dogs, eh?

Like I said, the team was all jumbled up, completely tangling the gangline. I had to take every dog off the line, tie them to a stump, tree, or the sled (eighteen dogs), and straighten the whole business out. Before I hooked everybody up to go on to Skwentna, I put a chain I had brought along on that front snow hook in place of the old rope before I stowed it in the sled. I didn't have any more problems like that.

The run up the Yentna River during the day was smooth. The dogs and I had been on the same trail only a month before on the Knik 200. A mile or so from Yentna Station, an inn, I started seeing signs that said "Free"… "Mushers"… "Food"… "Coffee"… "Waffles." That sounded to me like a great place to stop and soup the dogs. As I pulled in, I noticed another driver having trouble convincing her team to leave. I did my dogs, went inside and ate, and when I came back out, she was just rounding the bend. It took me a while to get ready to go, and as I rounded the first bend, I drove by that same poor musher a dozen yards or so off the trail with a balled up, fighting team.

It is another testament to the dogs and training that I was able to 'Gee' (turn right) and 'Haw' (turn left) my team in and out of checkpoints at will. The checkers are always wanting to run out and grab a musher's leaders to guide a team into a parking place. Many times I left them standing gape-jawed as I voice-maneuvered the team wherever I wanted to park. That was pretty fun.

One of the other things that got people to looking was when we were ready to go. I'd get whoever was around to come over and tell them to "Watch this. This is my favorite part." The dogs would be all laid out resting and I would zip up the sled bag and say "Get Ready!" They would all pretty much instantly get up, look around, and start barking and whining. Toward the end of the race, they maybe didn't get up quite as fast, or get too excited, but the command was a good cue that we were about to get moving again.

The run up the Yentna River to the Skwentna Roadhouse checkpoint was pretty easy – pretty much the last easy run for hundreds of miles. We got to the first real checkpoint sometime in the evening. I did the checkpoint routine for the dogs and wandered around talking to other mushers. I was still pretty excited, and not feeling much like sleeping. I didn't want to eat, and I don't think I drank much either. That's where my trouble started.

I decided to get on the road shortly after midnight. For the first time since training, I had the dogs hooked up in their real traveling configuration; fast dogs up front, big strong dogs next, the take-it-easiers and smaller dogs toward the middle-back, and the good wheelers (last dogs in line that steer the sled) next to the sled. For the first day, the plan was to really travel slowly so I had the team almost reversed. By now, the dogs were settled down enough to pull smart, and I had them set up for Full-Speed-Ahead.

The team went like this: Emitt, a ten-year-old leader, and Tatters (named for the wreck he left of some equipment early in life), my eighteen-month-old wonder were in lead. Big white Beaver and smaller brown Nutria, kin to Tatters, were my fine swing dogs (a second set of leaders). Blackbeard, a grey three-year-old from Martin's training program, and young blue-eyed Joe rounded out my "front end." Big dogs Larry and Eric (the Red) were next. Ten-year-old Jim Cooper (my ace in the hole for blizzards) and Six-Foot Louie rounded out my power section (although Coop didn't pull fifty miles the whole race, that not being his job). Smaller, steady workers Big Girl, Greta, Dingo, Christie, Cleopatra, and Genevieve filled up the gangline. Super wheel dogs Curly and Isabella topped off a fine string. When we pulled out of the checkpoint, I was off on one of the best and worst times I would have on that Iditarod.

The trail from Skwentna to Finger Lake leaves the river and winds its way up through the foothills of the Alaska Range. We left under a bright moon with a cold, hard trail under us, fairly ideal night-mushing conditions. Along about two in the morning I switched off my head light, put a light foot on the drag, and let the dogs cruise. After a short flat stretch, the trail starts to wind upwards.

This was the best time. The trail twists up and down, around hair pin turns, banks between rocks and trees, always heading up. I was amazed at the team's performance (my own included). We couldn't make a wrong move. The dogs went like a freight train. Most of the time I couldn't see more than two or three pairs of dogs for the winding trail. My leaders may have been going uphill in a turn to the left, dogs a few back might be in a turn to the right, dogs still farther back would be going through a dip in a stream bed, and I'd be following with the sled snaking between a big rock and some birch trees.

There are many ways a musher can apply force on the back end of the sled to get that long, straight contraption to go where it's supposed to. Some times I'd be pivoting the sled around a corner on the tip of the inside runner. Other times I'd be power sliding the back end around, or horsing the handlebar to bend the whole shebang. There are probably around two dozen things a musher can do with his weight and muscles to maneuver the sled, and for that trail it was all of them that I knew, all of the time.

That was the greatest. Under a bright moon, I couldn't see where the trail went, but counted on the dogs that I couldn't see to go the right way and not screw around and get tangled up. The dogs (wheelers excepted) couldn't do anything about steering the sled, but were powering along full steam ahead like they knew everything was in sync and they wouldn't get jerked to a sudden stop when the two-legs wrapped the sled around a tree. That was truly a fine run, the kind that comes around once in hundreds of miles. All too early the sun was full up and we had been on the trail for four hours. Time to stop and soup and snack.

That's when I ran out of gas and started to crash. I stopped at a burnt out party pit they tell me is at a place called Shell Lake. We had been on the run for about four hours, and I decided it was time to pull over. Half way into that procedure, I remember beginning to feel weak. I remember not wanting to heat up any of the food I had packed for myself; I'd just munch at Finger Lake. Not too far into the run after snacking the dogs, I started getting dizzy and trembly. It seemed like the trail was going on forever as I got weaker and weaker. It got so that all I could do was hang on the sled and watch the hallucinations. As I skipped in and out of consciousness, trees, shrubs, and rocks became couches, quarterbacks, toasters, and all kinds of things. That seemed to go on for a while, and then I got too weak to do anything but hang on. Eventually the dogs stopped for some reason or another, going up a hill, and I had to lie down for a while. It was all I could do to get up to the front of the team and tie the leaders to a tree, and unsnap the rest of the tug-lines on the way back. Then I put my shades on, fell on my sled, and slept.

Finger Lake

I slept for a while until some snowmachiners came up the trail and asked me what was up. I told them I couldn't go any more right now, but I was OK. They said 'all right' and left. I slept some more. I finally got up with enough energy, hooked up the team, and hung on 'til the Finger Lake checkpoint, an hour-and-a-half further down the trail. I got there and told the checker and the vet that the dogs were fine, but I was in a bad way. Did they have any Tang? I told them that I was dehydrated, starving, and barely conscious. I told them I wanted to take care of my dog team, eat, drink, and sleep.

After they brought me two jugs of water, I drank one down right quick, and promptly threw it back up. I figured that was going to happen, but it sent the checkers and the vet to scratching their heads. I didn't think I was in too bad a shape. I knew I had made myself sick, and all I had to do was eat and sleep, and take care of the team for as long as it took me to get back together.

The checkpoint routine, which I did several times getting back up to speed in Finger Lake, goes like this. Stop the team in the right place, with or despite the well meaning actions of the checkers and various people hanging around. Hopefully grab a bale of straw on the way by, or unsnap all the tug lines, hook the front of the team down, and go get a bale. Then flake out a nice bed of clean straw for each dog, kicking the last team's turds, spilt food, and trash out of the way. Take off the booties. If you're smart, you've already got a couple tubes of ointment and you goop some on every foot after giving every one of those feet a looking over on the way back from the leaders. Now you're back at the sled, and you pull out your bowls, cooker with stuff made up from the last stop, lots of broth, and the ladle and feed each dog. Then you go back, feeding the fast eaters more, and maybe take up the food from the holdouts (they'll be hungry later and eat well). Now get some water and make a fire in your cooker and plop in a meal or two for yourself. Try and feed the finicky ones again with a chunk of lamb or sausage or whatever that you're handing out on the way up the team again. Then try to get them to drink again. A good massage for everybody on the way back, and by now the vet is around looking at your dogs and Vet Book.

By the time everybody is on the same page on how the dogs are doing, your food is about ready and you slurp it down and put some more dog food in the hot water you just poured into the other cooler, for later. A last massage or brushing or wrist wrap or whatever they need, and it's time to head to where the people are and start sleeping or hanging out. Three or fours later, quietly repack the sled, and change runner plastic, then wake the dogs up gently putting booties on and massaging them up again, making them feel special, hand out a snack, and say "Git Up Doggies". Don't forget to pick up the trash and used booties and extra gear and get that in the pile to ship back to HQ.

For kicks, here at Finger Lake, I switched the satellite tracker message selector to "Hurt, but don't send help." I ended up taking two six hour sleeps, I think, and by the time twenty-one or so hours had gone by, I was ready to go again. The dogs were well and rested for the run down to the Happy River and up through Rainy Pass, the top of the world.

The trail to Rainy Pass was pretty fun. Several STEEP downhills with switchbacks at the bottom of them. Most even had hand-drawn warning signs. I guess these hills are infamous for wrecking people, but we had no trouble. They are the infamous Steps. The stay overnight in the checkpoint was uneventful. A vet doctored up an old burn wound of mine with super glue and mole skin when it was time to go. That's what we do to dogs' feet, and it worked great on my finger. So I left in the predawn darkness and headed up the Alaska Range.

It was UP... UP... UP... and UP some more all morning. The day was clear and cold, and it seemed like we were going across the top of the world. The only thing a musher can see at that level is mountain tops. Every thing else is much further below. That was a pretty neat feeling. Then we went over one last ridge, and we were headed down. That was to become one of the points that was really driven home on this Iditarod. Every time a musher goes UP one of those hills, there's a DOWN just like it pretty close by. The DOWN on the other side of the Alaska Range is the Dalzell Gorge, which is notorious for wrecking things.

The trip down to the Rohn River seems to be two sections, and the second is the Gorge proper. I was slipping and sliding down the first, easy part thinking "This ain't too bad at all." I was thinking "I had the terrible Dalzell Gorge whipped." Then I took another right, reached out to slap a tree on the way by, and whoops, I'm sitting in the snow watching my sled and dogs careen down this impossibly steep, one-hundred yard hill, sans me. This was the beginning of the Gorge. I caught up to the team at the turn at the bottom of the hill. The sled had flipped over into some alders, and fortunately stopped them. Somewhat chagrined, and more attentive, I continued on.

This section of the trail is truly a steep, rocky gorge with a frozen river running down the middle. We had to cross the river several times, going back and forth from one side of the gorge to the other. The catch is that the river ice is full of holes, and the whole shebang seems to be slanted down-hill so that whenever the sled hits the ice, it slides sideways. That made for some exciting, crashing and booming escapes from ice holes, and one good whack right into one.

A lot of times, I was able to pop the front end of the sled up and crash out of the hole, but this last time the sled slid in sideways and flipped over. The running river was about three feet under the ice shelf in these places, and I was thrown into the rocks and chilled water under the ice there. I smashed my head on the ice hole lip, but luckily retained consciousness. I scrabbled out of the river and back up onto the ice to find my sled with the front end jammed up under the lip. I thought it was totaled. And I was soaking wet.

Rohn

So I had to strip off my boots and wring out the liners, and shuck my pants to do the same with them (easy to do with that great Northern Outfitters gear). Then I chopped my sled out of the ice to find it undamaged. Like I told the TV news guys at Rohn River Checkpoint, "I guess Martin builds a tough one." From there it was a short, cold ride out onto the river glare ice and up to the checkpoint cabin. I spent about ten hours there drying out and tightening up my rig before heading out to the Farewell Burn, the toughest part of the whole race trail.

You begin to believe that you can be 'in tune' with nature, but it can be a set up for a sucker punch. You are always at odds with the elements, you go out on the trail, and you can get hurt.

People at the checkpoint had advised me not to spend the night and go out with a fresh team, since this part of the trail (the Post River / Farewell Lakes section) was really tough this year. Too eager dogs trying to go too fast would cause problems. So I left about an hour before dark with most of the dogs' tuglines unhooked. This negates ninety percent of a dog's pulling power, and I thought it would give me more control going downhill. I don't know if it helped at all since getting through that piece of trail turned out to be the hardest thing I have ever done in my life. There was little to no snow covering the frozen ground, and it took me six hours to get through twenty miles of frozen mud, steep, narrow, side-hilling, shale outcropping, hairpin-turned, boulder strewn, tree filled trail.

Leaving the checkpoint is not too bad. The trail is mostly flat, and though it was not a nice, snowy trail, it was doable, and before too long I hooked up the tuglines. One memorable section is a frozen waterfall that the dogs had to scrabble up. I guess it is a small, frozen creek, but they call it the Glacier, about thirty feet high. Twenty or thirty feet up in a team's length. It seems that a survey line is cut through about perpendicular to the actual trail, which goes up the Glacier. I thought the survey cut was the way, but the dogs knew the trail went straight up, since they smelled about a thousand dogs having gone that way, so that's the way we went.

The team, all hundred feet or so of it scrabbled and scraped its way up, towing me behind. They gravitated to the left side of the frozen creek, where there was some minimal purchase once they got up the waterfall. The trail goes to the right after you get on top. As the front of the team went back on the frozen stuff, they started slipping and sliding around, while the guys in back still had some purchase on the wrong side, so naturally they got all bunched and tangled up. The hundred-foot team was wadded up into about half that by the time the front was back on solid ground. So, it was stop, unsnap most of the guys, and straighten things back out. That all was kind of exciting and interesting, but no trouble. Nothing like what was to come.

Now we really started down the north foothills of the mountain range that was so fun to motor up a day or so before. This is what they call the Buffalo Tunnels. No snow this year, just frozen dirt, rocks, and stumps. Three times my drag ripped off catching on a stump as I stood on it to keep the speed down. Twice I stopped the team with a snow hook catching a tree, tied everybody to a shrub, went back and got the drag, and tied it back on. This year, like most of the training season, it was attached to the back stanchion with poly rope. The third time I was so frustrated at it ripping off, that I kept on going. Major mistake.

On the frozen ground, the brake, which is made to dig into snow, has no effect whatsoever on speed. It just beats the heck out of a guy's feet and legs as it smashes over rocks and stumps. That's the easy part. The hard part is it has no effect on speed. Now with no speed control, and no snow to steer the sled with, all a guy is left with is brute force horsing the sled around to keep from smashing into trees. Pretty quick I was sweating up a storm and cursing to beat the band. I had a long way to go like that.

That trail turned out to be one of the hardest physical and emotional things I've ever done. Even with the tug lines once again removed, the dogs knew I was excited, so, so were they. Unfortunately, I was struggling terribly, but they were screaming along having a blast, feeding off my emotion, just missing out on the notion that their joy and thrill was not what they were sharing with me. Several times I was unable to dodge the edge of a drop off, and while the dogs made it around a particular turn, me and the sled slid twenty or so feet down pulling the works to a halt. I couldn't get my boys to pull the heavy sled up to the trail, so I had to unload it, carry the junk back up to the trail, heave the sled up (with finally a little help from the team), get it stopped and secured, go back and get our junk and reload, knowing I hadn't a prayer of avoiding a repeat sometime in the near future. Sure enough, three times I think I missed the trail and had to do the manual labor routine. These were in between sweating buckets and cursing up a stream fighting to keep my uncontrollable sled in one piece and following the dogs.

I don't really have words to explain how mentally and physically beat I was, and the trail kept going like that for what seemed like forever. I remember thinking that if there was a checkpoint in the middle of that, I'd have given in and scratched. More likely, I'd have borrowed another drag and kept going, but fighting that trail had me thinking only of quitting. Only there was no where to go but back the same hell-trail I'd just been on. It was really bad. So we kept going as the afternoon turned into night and gradually got to where there was some snow again and it wasn't mostly down-hill, and the work load decreased mightily. I found myself glad that there was not in fact a checkpoint halfway through the Buffalo Tunnels. It was five hours or so of incredible effort and misery, but it, like my last malfunction leaving Skwentna, it passed.

Along about midnight, after the going had been pretty smooth for a while, I decided it was break time and pulled off to camp along side the trail. I slept 'til seven, got on the road around nine, and made Nikolai around five in the afternoon. The Farewell Burn proper, sixty miles or so of burnt spruce trees, blasted land, and blowing snow drifts, wasn't too bad itself. A lot of people up here think I got lost in the Burn. For the record, I never left the marked trail, and always knew where I was going. It just took me a long time. What took me twenty-three hours to do, Martin did in eight, with a one hour break included. Ninety miles.

Throughout the morning, as I'd look behind me, I'd see the Alaska Range sinking down into the horizon. That really gave me a sense of distance. It didn't seem like we were going very fast, but I realized that we must really be covering some miles. I knew what it took to get up and over those mountains. I knew they were big. As I watched them gradually disappear, I gained a new appreciation of how far we were traveling. I should have taken pictures, but my camera broke down two days before the start. Most ordinary lives don't offer that kind of vista, and Iditarod is special on that account. What would, years later, take me about ten minutes to fly over on the way to my job on an oil rig on the North Slope was the better part of a day at ground level watching Denali's brothers sink behind me.

When we were about two hours out, some snowmachiner passersby occasioned another high point of the race for me. I had been listening on my Walkman to some music, some mellow Jimmy Buffett, I think, and singing along to the dogs. With nothing better to do, I had been traveling like that for almost a whole tape. The snowmachiners came down on us from up the trail, and I stopped to chat. As soon as I had set the hook and started to talk, the dogs all began howling back at me.

The snowmachiners trying to talk to me were pretty amused, and even more so when I told them how I had spent the last half-hour singing to the dogs. The dogs were returning the favor. Either that or they were telling me how bad my singing stunk.

I took my mandatory thirty hour layover in Nikolai, a nice mid-to-large sized village in the interior, and all I can say about that time is my dogs ate a lot of lines. They were fat, happy, and bored. I was tired, beat, and bored. I fixed a few things on my sled, and waited 'til I could depart, at twelve-thirty-something the next morning.

McGrath, via the Kuskokwim River, was next.

This run turned out to be one of the coolest experiences I've ever been through. It was another clear, cold early morning departure. I figured I'd drive all night, and get into McGrath sometime in the morning, after sun-up. The trail gets on the Kuskokwim River shortly after leaving Nikolai. It follows the twists and turns of the river, all the way to McGrath, often going overland to cut off a bend in the stream.

I was fully rested, so I didn't worry that the head games my senses ended up playing with me were any problem. Lots of people sometimes get in that trance when they drive a car at night, where they all of a sudden realize that they've come five miles from the last time they can remember driving. That sort of thing happened to me, on a different scale.

I knew all the time that I was driving the sled, over the river, up and down the banks, and even on the twisty, tree-tunnel trail overland, but I was in a trance most of the time. It didn't seem like time was going by. I don't remember thinking about anything during those stretches. I guess awareness of each second of those runs was replaced by the next, with no immediate memory of the preceding. It was strange. I'd float out of that state to have a smoke, or eat something. I had to re-booty the team once after a water crossing. Then I'd slide back into that mental limbo. At first, I was scared that I was falling asleep at the wheel. Later when I realized that I wasn't, I let it do its thing, and got on down the trail. I made the checkpoint as the sun was coming up in front of me. The checker there was a pretty nice guy.

With Beaver.
photo: Kathy Chapoton

THE MIDDLE

I took a shower that morning (my second of the race), and talked with some other mushers I had caught up with. Since getting sick early on in the show, I had been traveling pretty much alone. McGrath was where I started traveling with and talking to other people again. It had been pretty cool with just me and my dogs, the last few days, but I was happy to catch up with some company.

I had another sled cached in McGrath, but all I took I think was a little fresh gear, and of course, the drag. Drags are good. Never drive a dogsled without one. Mostly the racer doesn't need it, though I kept a light foot on it most times, not being a racer, but when I needed it bad and left it behind on purpose, life got real bad real quick for a real long time. Mistakes on purpose are bad, bad, bad. Like all mistakes we learn from though, it gets put behind, and life goes on. So did the Iditarod miles.

Three or four of us left that afternoon, within a half hour of each other for Takotna, a town halfway to Ophir, the checkpoint where the Iditarod splits for its Northern and Southern routes.

The dogs and I had a fine run up, down, and around through the afternoon. One time coming down a hill, I fell over and tore down a big dead spruce tree with my body. I had a big bone bruise on my forearm for months after the race from that. Eventually we pulled into Takotna, twenty-some miles away, at the base of some mountains, for dinner. Takotna, if you ask me, is the nicest place on the whole race trail. It's small, clean, has a beautiful view, and is full of nice people who love the Iditarod. They always have hot water on a fire for the mushers, and a hall full of cakes, pastries, soups, and drinks, complete with a short-order kitchen. I souped the dogs, and went in for a bite. I ended up going back out and making my pups a full meal, then went back in and pigged out myself. I watched the TV news and signed some programs, and figured I'd make Ophir sometime in the dark, then run the ninety miles straight to Iditarod, the half-way point.

Now seems like a good place for a few words on the dogs. Up to this point I have been somewhat preoccupied with myself and the trail. All those experiences and feelings were new to me. Running a team of fine dogs, which was not new to me, got kind of overshadowed at times by what was happening to me. The dog team was always there, performing flawlessly. Imagine, as I have, driving a fine sports car for a long time. An old Datsun Z car or a new Mitsubishi GT. The machine is always there, dripping effortless power and strength. Same thing with the dogs. Their breeding, training, ability, and drive turned heads from Anchorage to the Coast (they got kind of tired long about White Mountain). They never quit, never balked, and never were not ready to go when I said we needed to.

Emitt and Tatters were still in lead, and Curly still headed up the wheel dog section. All the way from Anchorage, that is. We left Takotna late in the afternoon and climbed up, in, and around this mountain range, 'til we got to the other side and dropped into the Ophir checkpoint for the night.

The Ophir checkpoint is a cabin run by some very nice ladies and a man. They cook the mushers good hot meals, bring us water for our dogs, share the floor with us, and have a really nice little outhouse in back. One thing I remember in Ophir was when we were all crashed out, late at night. I remember having a nice dream about scratching my white dog, Beaver. As I gradually woke up, for some reason or another, I discovered that I was scratching the white-haired head of one of the ladies. Later when I told another Iditarod musher friend about it, he told me he had done the same thing a couple of times too. I petted people in my sleep as if they were my dogs two or three times this race, near as I can recall. Once at Tripod Flats, and at least once somewhere else.

Iditarod

The run to Iditarod was a long one. We made it without stopping to sleep in right at twelve hours. The first half of that run was pretty strange. We spent five hours going along the sides of these mountains at about a twenty degree starboard list. No trees, except for a few gullies, no nothing, just slanted snow. The second half was a pain. One after another, long steep rolling hills. We made camp about halfway, and I fed, checked, and rested the dogs for four hours. Eventually, in the pitch black night, we finished the long haul to Iditarod, the halfway checkpoint.

They say Iditarod is a ghost gold-town out there, but all it was for me was a broken down cabin in the middle of the night. I did have a little excitement there as I had packed myself a McDonald's meal in my drop bag. I threw it in the cooker like I do all my food, and in no time I had a juicy, tasty, bacon double cheese burger. The fries were kind of wet, but the sandwich and the cherry pie were great. They were a welcome break from six-hundred miles of pizza and sautéed shrimp over pasta.

All I remember about the run west to the Shageluk checkpoint is lots of those hills. The dogs walk up, and the musher drives down. Over, and over, and over, and over. Shageluk itself was a very nice checkpoint. The mushers I was traveling with and I had planned to get up and go at three or four in the morning. Of course we slept in 'til dawn, and got rolling about nine. We figured, "anyway, the dogs benefited from the rest." The going flattened out somewhat as we headed down toward the Yukon River.

Anvik is the first checkpoint on the Yukon River. I didn't really like the run up the Yukon. I did it mostly at night, two nights, and both times I had to pull over and sleep on the sled bag 'til light because I was falling asleep on the runners. I could just picture myself waking up by falling on the snow, watching my sled cruise on up the river. That was kind of a drag. Also, something about the atmosphere of the villages on the river rubbed me the wrong way. There were some genuinely kind and generous people at those places, but I wasn't getting good vibes.

It was a quick run from Shageluk to Anvik, a cold headwind all the way, and we didn't stay long there. It was only another four or five hours straight up the river to Grayling, and there was some question about the condition of the drop-bag supplies, so none of us wanted to stay too long. The run to Grayling was through a nice afternoon, and we made the village by early evening. The dogs were pretty pumped after a short, quick, easy run up the river. When I got to the village, one of the checkers convinced me that my dogs looked so good I should not spend the night, but keep going with them. Mistake. It cost me a dog.

We were ready to leave around eleven pm with no sleep for ourselves and little rest for the dogs. As soon as I left, I noticed my super-wheeler, Curly, limping badly. Before I had gone two miles, I turned around, went back to Grayling and dropped my first dog. I had kept all eighteen way past the halfway point, and started thinking that I could finish with them all. It broke my heart to leave my boy behind, but we had seventy miles to go before the next big break, and he was hurting.

Like I said, I was tired, tired, tired, and decided I was going to sleep on purpose, or do it by accident. So I pulled over, stripped booties, snacked the dogs, unsnapped the tug lines, and got comfortable on the sled with Six Foot Louie, who was kind of stiff. Lloyd Glibertson came by and woke me up around sun-up. We made Eagle Island two hours later. The Eagle Island homestead, where the checkpoint is, turned out to be a welcome oasis of comfort and hospitality. I, my traveling companions, and the dogs all enjoyed our brief stay there.

I think there were three Iditarod teams there, and a lady recreational musher driving from Kotzebue to somewhere in the interior and back. Mushers could sleep in a "lower" cabin, a nice, two-short-story affair, and eat in the main building. The owner's cook cooked for us too. The prettiest checker in the whole race and her helper were on hand to make sure things went smoothly. It sure was pleasant to have that college-girl checker come and deliver my wakeup calls. The second time, I missed her as Lloyd Gilbertson woke me up instead, and I went out to get ready to leave. I mentally kicked myself for hundreds of miles for not watching snoring Lloyd leave, then closing my eyes, and waiting for that pretty checker.

Kaltag

So, Eagle Island was pretty fun. Most of us back-of-the-packers left the checkpoint sometime in the early night. Once again I almost fell asleep, and pulled over to rest. Again Lloyd woke me and we continued on to Kaltag, the last checkpoint on the Yukon. Just after dawn, we could see the lights of the town on the left-hand bank. For some crazy reason, the marked trail zigged and zagged back and forth across the river so that it took us almost an hour to go that last five or six hundred yards. I was kind of aggravated about that situation then, when I popped up over the bank to find a town asleep in the early morning. There was no checker there, so I just kept going, figuring that the dogs could catch the scent of the trail and lead me to the checkpoint. Instead, the dogs smelled other dogs in the doglots of Kaltag, and led me on a high speed run all over town. We went through dog yards, front yards, back yards, over snow berms, and between houses. I think we got every dog in the village barking by the time the checker had chased us down. He didn't know how to get to the checkpoint from where we were, so we (me, the dogs, and Lloyd's team, since he had shown up by then) waited for him to find his way to where we were supposed to go, and come back and lead us there. The whole arrival was pretty funny. Lloyd and I had a good laugh waiting for our guide.

After taking care of the team, minus Curly, I lay down in the drop-dog straw and got a couple hours of good sleep. When I woke up, my traveling companions were talking to the trail sweep (snowmachiner official race followers) about how the weather was coming in, and we had better go.

The dogs were still doing great, I wished I could rest them some more, but I knew a good snow storm could really shut a musher down, and bury the race trail under three to four feet of fresh, drifted snow. The going would be extra tough then, so those of us in a position to do so followed the trail sweeps, now our trail breakers, out of Kaltag in the afternoon, headed for Unalakleet, on the coast.

The trail to Unalakleet is almost ninety miles, almost due west, toward the coast. Another long one. Big wet snowflakes began to fall as the team stretched out and shook themselves off for the run. By the time we got rigged out and ready to go, it was late in the evening, and the snow storm was getting worse. It had snowed off and on all the way since we got on the Yukon, days ago. The dogs did not seem to be too bothered by the weather yet. Snow that added an extra layer of complication to my driving just fell onto and shook off of the moving dogs. Halfway in between Kaltag and Unalakleet, on the left side of the trail, is a BLM (Bureau of Land Management) shelter cabin where we figured to spend the night. So, we mushed on through the snowy evening, through an ever deepening and deteriorating trail. I stopped once, about four hours out, and fed the dogs some warm soup that I had made in Kaltag, and pushed on 'til I heard dogs barking and saw the reflectors of the side trail to the cabin.

Lloyd Gilbertson, Harry Caldwell, the female recreational musher and I all parked, fed, and bedded down our teams in parking trails that our trail sweeps had laid down. I think there were three trail sweeps, so that made for a pretty cozy space, outside of the elements. We BSed for a while and a few of the mushers drank some whisky. We had a good rest, and straggled out in the morning toward Unalakleet.

It took six or more hours to get there, and sometime during the run I had stopped to cook my dogs a little hot meal. The recreational team caught up to me, and as I was talking to the lady from Kotzebue, I showed her my satellite tracker thing. Of course I didn't notice that I had flipped the Emergency switch before I re-stowed it.

With Tatters, the young star of Iditarod XXI.
photo: Kathy Chapoton

THE END

When I got to town, I saw a lot of people waiting on the incoming trail. When I pulled up, they all were asking "What was the matter?" "Where was the musher in trouble?" It took them a while to figure out that I was that guy, and I took a while figuring out what they were so agitated over. Then I got the Argus out, flipped off the switch, and put it back. We all shook our heads, for different reasons, and went back to work. Word had gotten to Martin in Nome that I had hit the Scratch button and was in trouble. He was burning up the lines wondering why a rookie musher was forty miles behind the trail sweeps, and what was going on.

When I debriefed with the tracking guys, we discussed the need for a more positive safety cover for that critical switch. Both I and the other musher carrying the device accidentally turned the emergency beeper on. Imagine if all sixty-nine mushers had one. The relay satellite would probably burn up and fall out of orbit.

Lloyd Gilbertson, Harry Caldwell and I got a pleasant surprise as soon as we parked in Unalakleet. The dozen or so other mushers that had pulled away while we slept our way down the trail were all jammed up in town suffering through a race freeze. It seems that a storm had blown in from the sea, as is the norm in that part of the state, and the drivers were under the impression that they could not continue until the storm went away. Depending on who you ask, you get different answers on how long the race was officially frozen at that point on the trail. Some of the mushers there, though, had been there sitting on their thumbs for almost three days.

The teams were all parked along some roads around the gym where the mushers were quartered. While the area was clear of litter, and generally policed, it was easy to tell that they had been there for a while. Dogs were growling and snapping at each other, everybody had chewed lines hanging off of ragged ganglines, and the snow and spilt food was trampled down as flat as concrete. Inside, those who were not playing basketball or rearranging their gear were complaining about how long they were having to sit. My traveling companions and I had many good chuckles about how we were now back with all those back-of-the-pack "racers."

The low point of that stay was when I had to drop my second dog before I left. Big black, shaggy Larry, Curly's brother (Moe didn't make the run) turned up lame in a hind leg, and the vet said, and I agreed, that he should be dropped. He is fine now, and knows he did a good job for as long as he could.

In the morning, the storm was over, the race official said we could go, and the trail sweeps went out to break us a trail up over some tall hills and along the beach to Shaktoolik. Once off the hills, I broke out my little sail, rigged it up on the fly, and headed toward the next checkpoint on a nice starboard beam-reach.

Nobody in our group stayed long in Shaktoolik. It was mid afternoon, and we all figured that we'd take a good break at Koyuk, some eight hours north of Shaktoolik over the Norton Bay sea ice. Most of that run was in the middle of the night. Many of those mushers, me included, think we had wolves traveling along with us just out of headlamp range. For half an hour or so, the dogs were all sniffing to the right, occasionally yipping, and generally looking very interested about something I couldn't see.

It takes forever to get over to Koyuk. You can see the lights of the village for hours. It is depressing and frustrating that they never appear to come any closer. During this run, two dogs, Big Girl and Genevieve, started running funny and looking hurt. I ended up loading Genevieve in the bag, which she greatly appreciated, for the last hour. After the vet saw them, we discovered that they both had some sore muscles; Genevieve a bicep, and Big Girl a quadriceps. The vet lady said both would probably have to be dropped in the morning, but that I should massage them with Ben-Gay, and wrap them up in dog coats and wrist wraps to keep them warm, and maybe one could make it. So that's what I did, for an extra forty-five minutes that night, and again in the morning. I could tell Genevieve was flying out of this checkpoint as she was in a lot of pain. Big Girl recovered enough to continue, and eventually walk into Nome with me, though I gave her the treatment whenever we camped.

The night and the morning in the community center with all the other mushers was a kick. We had a lot of laughs, bitched back and forth about this and that, and stunk up the place for six or seven hours. I had convinced the others that how I had to drop dogs was by hurrying out of a checkpoint when I knew the dogs were using the rest. Curly at Grayling, Larry hurrying to beat the storm into Unalakleet, and now almost two dogs pushing on out of Shaktoolik with no sleep. So, the group slept in late and started trickling out some nine or ten hours after arriving. This was long for some other people, and long for some other people's plans, but I don't think it cost anybody anything to stay and sleep, while letting their dog teams do the same.

Next stop Elim. It was a short, cold ride to there, and the team and I arrived in the late afternoon. The checkpoint seemed to be on the beach, with the town a horseshoe above. Lots of kids were running around, and a group of them decided to hang out around my sled. I quickly enlisted them to fetch me this and that from around the checkpoint. I figured that since we were supposed to get along with the locals, I'd let them help if they wanted to. However when I turned around expecting to see them carrying me a case of HEET (fuel for the cooker) and a bucket of water, I saw the checker walking toward me instead with the kids in tow. "No help," he said, and the kids were relegated to just watching.

By now, since I did not switch to a smaller sled in Unalakleet, I started thinking that the one my team was pulling was getting pretty heavy. I emptied it out, banged and scraped off at least a dozen pounds of encrusted ice, and began to throw stuff in return bags. Bullets, my frying pan, two pair of lineman's pliers, and twenty or so extra brass snaps went into the bag right quick. I dug through my personal bag and threw out all the extra socks, gloves, face masks, hats, batteries, matches, medicines, tapes, books (to write in, that I never did), and all the junk that had been accumulating there for the last thousand miles.

Wet boot liners, extra knives, one-hundred feet of rope, a big tarp, and my roll of toilet paper (booties work better); they all got sent home here. Candy bars, sandwiches, other hoarded grub, and paper trash got the axe too. I also cleaned off a dozen or so chewed-off neckline and tugline ends from my gangline. Since Unalakleet the dogs had been walking slower and slower, and I figured it was past time to lighten their load. I dropped around twenty pounds of stuff, and wished I could lose more. That three-pound brick of a satellite tracker was looking awful tempting, but I left it in.

An empty sled weighs in at around forty pounds, a loaded one around ninety. My two-and-a-half pound Northern Outfitters greatcoat also wanted to go, but I knew that if I really needed it in a storm on the coast here, and had thrown it out eight hours back, I'd be angry and in a bind. So that stayed. I should have dropped my gun too (four pounds), but I kept it.

(In '94, Martin and I would build me a smaller starting sled so I couldn't fit as much stuff in it, and I would switch to a smaller 'coastal' sled in Unalakleet.)

Elim, Golovin, White Mountain, Safety, Nome. We were about fifteen days out, and only one or two more to go.

I don't think anybody did more than set their hook in Golovin, sign the check sheets, maybe throw the dogs some cold snacks, and go. That's what I did. That village is in the middle of a fairly easy run from Elim to White Mountain. Also, it was blowing about thirty knots, and uncomfortably cold.

I don't remember too much about the trip to White Mountain. I think we drove along some big cliffs about a half mile offshore. The dogs were still tooling on down the trail pretty good. It sure seemed like we were crawling, barely moving, but the scenery was going by, the batteries in my walkman were still jamming, and the dogs' tails were still occasionally wagging.

White Mountain

We finally pulled into the town of White Mountain where all mushers take a mandatory twelve hour layover. For most mushers this is somewhat of an imposition. Most mushers gripe about having to spend so much time there, but for my dogs and me, and the few mushers I was traveling with, twelve hours was rushing things a bit. That was pretty funny there. My dogs got a clean bill of health from the vet during the mandatory vet check there. That felt pretty good. I also phoned home and talked to my Mom from the building where we stayed. We both got a charge out of that.

All too soon the clock ticked down and it was time for the last long run. Up and over the Topkok Hills, down to the Safety roadhouse, and on to Nome.

Memory gets kind of foggy about who left where, when, this late in the race, but my team was less than an hour in front of the next, and an hour behind the one ahead. Four or five of us spaced ourselves out like that going up to the hills. The Topkok Hills on the northwest corner of Norton Sound went up and up like none before on the race. The dawning sun followed us up, around, and over, on the sides and crests of these sharp, steep hills. We wound around these hills, always going higher.

In spite of being upwards-only, it really was a good run. The dogs had just gotten warmed up on the trail to the hills from a good twelve-hour regulation stop. They were slowly powering up the constant incline, no problem at all.

Presently we crested the final ridge and slid down to sea level again for the run westward to the last shelter cabin, and on to Safety. As the rising sun followed us down the hillside, visibility began to get poorer. We were driving into one of the cold remnants of the storm that had frozen the race not too long ago.

I didn't figure that at the time. The dogs and I were having such a cool morning run; all I knew was that I had to pull my goggles down over my eyes on account of the sharp, blowing snow. This, of course distorted my vision, color-wise, and I began to see the storm that I didn't know I was in in a new light. My goggles have an orange tint, and they combined with the morning sun, the blowing snow, and the starkness of the landscape to create a surreal, animated-like (Roger Rabbit in pastels) moving picture.

Most things were in shades of purple and blue. The ocean was south, not too far to my left, and the jagged crests of the sea ice were pointed swirling purple and violet. The Topkok Hills behind me were darker shades. The sun, over my right shoulder, was deep oranges and reds. The wind was constantly blowing off-shore, and while the snow we were traveling on was white, the further up forward I looked the mistier and bluer it became.

The whole effect was really bizarre, and really cool. I probably had some rock and roll going then, and I'm sure that added to the scenery. So, we were in this storm headed to a shelter cabin about halfway between the edge of the Topkok Hills and the Safety roadhouse.

There was no "trail", in the regular sense. Most of the trail markers (four foot wooden lath) were buried in the fallen snow so that only the top six or eight inches showed. The terrain was level for as far as you could see; there was no indented path for the eye to follow, but there were enough signs of the race trail so that between the dogs and me, we had no trouble. The trail markers marked the general path for me, and the dog-scent marked the way for the team. Usually, I could spot the hardest packed course as a raised ribbon in the soft, blowing snow, snaking in and out of the visible trail markers. I still had my head light running from the morning, and the reflectors at the top of the trail markers made a line of bright pin-pricks heading out a moving mile or so ahead of me. My leaders, Tatters and Emitt, and I shared the responsibility of keeping the team and sled out of the soft snow, and heading in the right direction… straight ahead.

Soon enough the coolness ended and we wove through some snow-sand dunes, with the wind howling all around us, and found ourselves at a small cabin on the high ground of a beach. There isn't much to say about the stay at the cabin. The cabin itself is a very handy thing, with some bunks and a big wood burner, but it was really cold outside. The walls are covered with notes written by whoever felt like writing. I wrote that I was there with my eighteen month old wonder dog Tatters. Either we stayed too long, or too short, because when I got the dogs up to go, they looked really cold and tired. I had given them a thick meat soup hot meal, and heated myself up some food inside, but I was glad we were nearing the end. So were the other few race mushers I ran into at the cabin. I think the two veterans in my team, Jim Cooper and Emitt, communicated some sense of impending relief to the young dogs as we got going on the last miles to Nome.

We drove out of the storm before too long, and spent the rest of the morning slowly walking along the coast 'til we hit the Safety roadhouse, the only structure visible for miles, around noon. The sun was shining, but it was still real cold as I fed the dogs some more thick warm soup, and all the cold snacks in my drop bags before having a couple of hot dogs and some OJ. Immediately thereafter, I put my official number 60 bib back on, tried the dogs on another snack, and moved out on the last stretch to Nome.

It was a long slow haul along the beach in the sunshine. The dogs were tired, and we were passed by a few of the teams that we had been traveling with since the shelter cabin. Along the coast, and around the headlands; all afternoon, slower and slower we mushed. Finally, Nome was in sight. By this time, three teams were in sight ahead of me.

Nome

The back side of Nome was a forest of trail stakes marking several local trails. The mushers in front of me, instead of going straight onto Front Street, turned off into that connect-the-dots of lath. Thirty minutes later, after going back and forth, around and backwards, behind Nome, a snowmachiner came out and two of us asked what was up. He told us we were in the wrong place, and we took off for the nearest street on the edge of town.

As soon as we got into Nome we picked up a police escort to lead us to Front Street on the other side of town. Joe Carpenter and I were one on the other's heels (me on his) as the Burled Arch came into sight. I tried to call Emitt to go 'on by' and pass him up, but the dog just looked back at me like I was crazy and just kept going on like he was. Emitt and Tatters crossed the finish line seventeen days, eight hours, and fifty-four minutes after taking off in Anchorage.

Emitt, Tatters, Joe, Nutria, Beaver, Blackbeard, Big Girl, Christie, Dingo, Greta, Isabella, Cleopatra, Louie, Eric, and Jim Cooper pulled me on the same sled over ELEVEN-HUNDRED MILES, through every terrain this state has. Curly, Larry, and Genevieve got the early ride home.

My Father, surprising me by coming up from Texas, was waiting for me just past the Burled Arch that marks the finish line. I sure was glad to see him. We spent two days in Nome, staying with a wonderful family before the flight back to Anchorage, and the world.

When the Iditarod is over… it's over. Unless a guy or gal wins the race, then when it's over it's back to life as previously normal. There are bills to pay, dogs and gear to get shipped home, a ton of stuff to clean and organize… life goes on and the musher has a little catching up to do. The purse may pay the entrance fee and the taxes and might buy some gear for next year. The rest of the world waits for the musher to catch up and get back with it. About the only lasting physical reminder, once the bruises are faded and the dogs are back to spinning around on their chains, is the mail. Mushers get boxes of mail from students, all of which should be individually answered. That lasts for six weeks or so, and as long as it takes to get it all answered. By the time that's all squared away and a guy is back in the groove and has taken a little vacation, it's time for the fall training routine again. The ultra competitive musher starts his appearances and dog-and-pony shows almost before his face is done peeling. Not for me though; it was back to scooping poop, playing with puppies, getting up in the morning and soaking dogs' feet, bla bla bla. Life as usual.

Iditarod gives you a lot of time to think about a lot of things. I learned about my sense of perspective, and scale; that these things are not absolutes. That there are other scales and perspectives to the world besides the personal.

At the Finish of Iditarod XXI.
photo: Charles Chapoton

With wind-burnt face and bandaged fingers, calling home from Nome.
It was wonderful to have such kind and generous hosts, Pat Hahn and
Sue Greenly, with such a comfortable house.
photo: Unknown

Back to work at Happy Trails.
photo: Kathy Chapoton

At the start of Iditarod XXII.
photo: Unknown

IDITAROD XXII

For me it was a pretty eventful race. In many ways it was harder than the first. Average temperatures well below minus ten, poor snow conditions, and relentless wind made most every run a painful struggle.

On the positive side, the limelight followed the team the whole way. I almost died at Finger Lake; the news media did that up big. My satellite tracker and a broken down lady musher put me in the news during the run through the Farewell Burn. Then, mushing through a ground storm into Safety put me next to tragedy, and back into the news. Then we got the last-place Red Lantern Trophy. The dog team, appropriately, got the last shot by setting the record for the fastest Red Lantern. Ever. At sixteen days, sixteen hours, and seventeen minutes, we broke the old record by nineteen hours. (As with most records, ours was soon broken.)

The team in '94 was twenty dogs. King (the only adult), Little Foot, Jimmy Buffett, Racket, Jamie, Tom, Chester, Orca, Beluga, Barracuda, Dolphin, Regatta, Whaler, Pirate, and Jib Sheet finished. *(Now, 2008, you can start with at most sixteen. Twenty is a LOT of dog power.)* They were beautiful. The team was so powerful, so fast, so cool. The race took a bit more than sixteen days, new challenges every time they woke up, on and on, time after time, and they kept plunging on, running through each situation, looking back, and running on. Five of my dogs had to be dropped during the race. Solo, my pet, went at Rainy Pass. He was the first. He developed a limp going into Finger Lake. Jill left from Nikolai, Endeavor from Ophir. Cortez went from Ruby. Lafite limped all down the Yukon and I dropped her at Nulato. Laird Barron finished with sixteen dogs, I had fifteen, everybody else had fewer.

I was constantly amazed by the dogs and their acts in harness. I watched them continue their learning and overcoming, episode after episode, as the miles went by. They were smoother, stronger, and faster then my first Iditarod team. Except for some steep mountains, they ran the whole way. That's in comparison to walking, lots of the time, for other teams. We clocked in-between-checkpoint times that made most other mushers look like they were crawling on their hands and knees.

Throughout the whole race I marveled at the dogs I ran with, and I'll try to show things from their perspective too. At least my perception of their perspective. So, even though I screamed at the mountains and the wind a thousand times that this was terrible, and I'd never do it again, I had a really great race.

THE BEGINNING

So, there was the Start (March 5, 1994) in Anchorage. I overslept that morning, waking up as Martin was loading his dogs and leaving. Our handy helpers had fed the animals earlier, and we had our gear packed to travel hours before; so I was able to just pull on some warm gear, supervise my team and equipment into the truck, and get on the road. Thankfully Jim Davis (handling my dogs, in his new dog truck) had some coffee, and I had all my papers in order, so I was able to relax on the trip to Anchorage. I don't think the pups knew what was up, but they sure knew something big was happening, and they were excited.

It was cold there, in the dark morning in Anchor Town. Minus twenty or so when we arrived. Quickly and coldly I stripped out of my handling clothes in the gear alley of the truck. I slipped into my full mushing suit and hung out with my dogs (still in their boxes on the truck), waiting on time to do things.

I left the dogs waiting, warm and comfortable, in their boxes until the drug testing crew came around. Even though only six dogs could run in the starting parade, all twenty had to make the trip so they could go before the testers. It was getting about time, so I had all my team put on the ground to wait some more as the testers collected urine from a few dogs. I took Solo, my pet, out first, and he was the first to provide a sample for the testers. I was a little worried about that since Solo drinks the occasional beer with me, but there was no problem. Testing for drugs in the canine athletes of the Iditarod is important to the race. Several classes of chemicals are banned, including stimulants, sedatives, analgesics, and steroids. Evidence of prohibited drugs in race dogs' systems brings heaps of trouble down on the musher. Sample collecting and analyzing prevents dogs being able to run past their natural limits.

So, no trouble there, as we waited some more. I petted my dogs, talked to some reporters. Talked to some fans, talked to my friends, and played with my gear to pass some more time. After some of the early teams, including Martin's, passed us on their way to the starting line, I had all but my starting six put back in the truck.

My team was bib number 37. That was our starting position, so after a few other teams had left, we harnessed up my six dogs and started moving up the chute. I had picked King, the adult, Solo, the pet, and four other dogs with the most potential for the parade team. King and Little Foot led, Jimmy Buffett and Regatta were behind them, and Solo and Lafite had the wheel honors. My small and light dog mushing friend, Lexi Hill, rode with us as handler as per race rules.

I was much more relaxed at the starting line this year, and had a really pleasant three mile ride through town. The dogs looked like they were having a blast. They still didn't know exactly what was up, but they knew how to run, and that's all they were supposed to be doing. There were lots of fans, no trouble, and it had warmed up with the sun. We finished the run, the truck met us at the end, the dogs went back in their boxes, and the sled went on the roof. On the way home our truck passed soon-to-be-ex-champion Jeff King's rig twice. That was Saturday. This was the first of the two-day start routine. A parade on Saturday, then the Race Clock starts Sunday.

The trip to Willow, the location of the restart the next morning, went as planned: the same twenty dogs, with more gear, in the same truck, and with more help. As we loaded up my sled for our final departure, one of my handlers broke the zipper on my sled bag. Luckily I had brought all my gear in a duplicate sled bag (minus sponsor patches), so we did the quick switcheroo and were ready to go. People tell me that I was a lot calmer during the Start this year, as opposed to last year. Even now, I find myself more accepting of sudden obstacles to my activities. I just deal with them, and go on (for better or worse).

The dogs were pretty hyped up during all this, of course, and I had some handlers detailed to stick with the team and comfort the agitated. That worked pretty well, and as the clock ticked down, and the early teams took off, again we hooked mine up. All twenty dogs.

Ten pairs of dogs makes for a pretty huge sled gangline. Not only in size (upwards of 100 feet), but in raw power. Sixteen race dogs routinely pull trucks around training, so you can imagine twenty. Several times during training, when we had good snow, I went out with full twenty-dog teams. I thought I had a pretty good handle on it, but was in for some surprises in the coming days.

Anyway, we taxied to the starting line, received the countdown, were released, and on our way. Fans, partying and camping, lined the trails and dotted the frozen lakes for the first few miles. It seems like some kind of Mardi Gras parade for them. Float after float speeds by, stirring up the party every few minutes. Mushers toss out trading cards or booties to those who ask, and everybody passes a good time. I don't know what they do after we are all gone. Truly, out of sight, out of mind.

Eventually the nice trail drops down onto the Susitna River for a brief run south where it catches the Yentna River for the run northwest to Skwentna. Along the way there is Yentna Station, a new official checkpoint this year, where most all the teams made their first rest stop.

I decided to make our stop about five miles before the checkpoint. It was snowing and blowing a little, so as I spied a sheltered section of the riverbank, I drove the team off the trail and made camp as the rest of the racers made their way on. For four hours or so, we relaxed and watched the teams go by. We also listened to wild barking in the distance as the teams at the checkpoint did their thing. In good time, I packed up shop, rubbed the dogs down, and got back on the trail. We made Yentna Station in another twenty minutes or so and passed right on through the teams lined out on the bank. Of course we went the wrong way into the checkpoint; barreling though the middle of the camp, (twenty hot dogs, full steam ahead) stopping only long enough to exchange pleasantries, check in, and check right back out.

Following an easy, but cold, run up the river, we landed at Skwentna sometime in the evening. I did the checkpoint routine with the dogs, ate, drank lots of Tang, and lay down in the cabin to sleep. Later, as my team was preparing to go, a lone racing team came down into the checkpoint from the wrong direction. It seems that this musher had missed a turn, and was pretty angry about ending up on the wrong trail – down a river not suitable for dog sled travel. He was pretty hot, and told his story for all those gathered 'round, so I figured to be watching for that spot and not miss the turn myself. King, my adult (maybe the only one of the twenty-one of us), actually led the team and me off of one trail, and over on to the correct one. "Thanks bud, no sweat." King is pretty hard headed, but a real good dog.

The trail to Finger Lake this year was pretty different from last year. Last time was a cold, hard trail night. This time it was light, and the traveling was through deep, new, wet snow (just about the only place on the race trail that way). I stopped occasionally to talk to a passer-by, or pet the dogs, but mainly just watched them pull the sled up through the snow. Like last year, we did stop for a regulation four-hour break at Shell Lake. No hallucinations this year though. No problem. The dogs continued to tool along, having a good time yipping and yapping back and forth at each other as we headed up through the falling snow into the foothills of the Alaska Range.

By this time the dog team had settled into their normal "racing" configuration. King and Little Foot led, as they had during the parade, and as they would for the whole race. (2008: Little Foot's next and last owner, Nancy Marty, still overflows with praise for that thirty-pound gray wonder dog.) Jimmy Buffett was the head swing dog, and he and his pal Orca were comfortable working together way up there. A few special dogs, Whaler, Jill, Jib Sheet, Pirate, and Barracuda, rotated in and out of this front section, and the wheel positions. They were good in any of those critical spots, and real assets to the team for their skill and versatility. Big, tall, rangy, black and white brothers Regatta and Endeavor, and brothers Jamie and Tom made up two big pairs in the middle of the team, although Regatta occasionally ran in front (a cross-eyed dog if you can imagine). Solo, Lafite, matched sisters Dolphin and Beluga, Cortez, Chester, and Racket (guess why he was named) filled out my core of working dogs.

After last year, I knew I wanted to be rotating dogs around in my team, and that worked out pretty well this year. Throughout the whole race, and with few exceptions, no dog ran in that tough wheel position twice in a row. Also, with few exceptions, all dogs got to do runs in less demanding positions than they are best running in. As individuals, maybe they were not always run to their potential, but as a team, I think they were.

This run up to Finger Lake went much smoother than on my first year. The snow was deep and wet, and the dog team powered its way up through the trees. It was pretty easy going for me, but a little harder for the dogs. All of the snowmachines and dog teams ahead of me had created deep holes in the trail snow. Many times my team would ripple-fall into those holes. The dogs didn't like that, and would often try to stay up on the trail by jumping out to the side, and stepping on the ledge. I could tell they were working hard. Even if the dog just let himself be pulled through the hole, it looked tough. More than one of my team members benefited from the early, long rest we ended up taking at that place, using that time to recover from the difficult trail.

You remember the troubles I dished myself out on that trail last year. This year, four other mushers and I almost died at the checkpoint at the end of that trail. Here is that story.

Finger Lake

The checkpoint at Finger Lake consisted, like last year, of a hillside where dog teams parked, a cabin which was off limits for sleeping to mushers, an airstrip on the frozen lake, and a Dodge Lodge for dropped dogs. The Dodge Lodges were half-pipe, insulated tents donated by Anchorage Chrysler Dodge's owner Rod Udd. Weather Port is a common brand name, and Dodge (a major sponsor of the Iditarod) had their name put on two dozen and flew them out to Iditarod checkpoints. They are handy to house sick and tired dogs out of the elements. Rumor had it that mushers before our group dragged in two propane heaters and took over the tent for sleeping quarters. It was still snowing heavy and wet, so the heated shelter was inviting, since the alternative was to sleep inside our sled bags.

My team pulled into the high lake checkpoint and was parked going up the hillside next to Bruce Moroney and Cathy Mormile. Jamie Nelson pulled in with her purebred show Malamutes after a while. My team ate what I served them and settled down to rest. All were looking good except for Solo, who was sore in the front, and Whaler, who was sore in the wrist. Everybody had dog coats on, and Whaler had a wrist wrap loosely warming his swollen joint.

I said good night to my dogs and carried my sleeping bag and dry boot liners into the warm Weather Port to find Bruce asleep, and Cathy just getting ready to lie down. I remember griping with Cathy about how we'd made the tent so airtight that water was dripping down from the condensation. I joked that we ought to cut a vent hole so some of our stuff could dry. By the time we got comfortable, Jamie and Lisa Moore came in and we all went to sleep. I remember feeling a splitting headache as I dozed off. Sometime later Cathy got up to see to her dogs and began stumbling around the tent. She started complaining about how her boot strap kept tripping her. I told her to cut it off, and we did. Then I went back to sleep.

The next thing I remember is dimly hearing somebody hollering that we had to get out, that we were being asphyxiated. The carbon monoxide generated by the propane heaters was killing us. I knew it was Jamie and she was serious, but all I thought was that I wished she would shut up so I could go back to sleep. It was strange. I understood her that we were being killed, but I was so warm and comfortable, almost asleep, that I just couldn't move. I remember hearing horrible wheezing noises from the others in the tent, and again wishing they would be quiet too because I was oh-so comfortable.

After I don't know how long, Jamie's message got through to me and I crawled to my knees and spent forever trying to get my jacket zipper together. Finally I stumbled out of the tent and smelled the fresh air. By that time, another musher or two and some checkpoint personnel had arrived and were looking to help. Bruce, Lisa, and Cathy had to be dragged out, unconscious. I spent some time slapping faces and shaking bodies trying to wake them up, but no-go.

I was very shaky on my feet, soaking wet, and shivering in the cold, so I figured to walk to the cabin, since that's where we were all going to end up. Like a fool, I decided I had to go get my gear from in the tent, since it would dry better in the cabin with me. The gas had been turned off, and the door opened, but as soon as I stepped in, I got twice as dizzy and stumbly and barely got out on my feet with my gear. Jamie and I started the long walk up to the cabin figuring to meet a snowmachiner along the way who would pick us up. As we saw the headlight coming on, I fell to my knees and waited there, drooling in the snow.

They took us all to the cabin, where they stripped us down and covered us up with blankets. I was kind of in the background, as most of the activity centered on the unconscious two. Bruce had come around by then, Cathy was making mumbling noises, but Lisa was still out like a light. Our rescuers began fashioning an oxygen tent for her out of a welding bottle and regulator, and a plastic trash bag. That was up and running in short order, and before too long she came around.

They wouldn't let me sleep, like I wanted to, so I lay there shivering. I listened to Cathy and Lisa throw up. Radiophone traffic was flying between our checkpoint personnel, race officials, and medical specialists. It seems that they like to put carbon monoxide poison victims in hyperbaric chambers to purge the deadly gas from their bodies. Luckily for us there is a six-hour window where that treatment is helpful, and we couldn't make it to a chamber in time. Since it was at night, and there were storms between here and there, Lifeguard couldn't fly us out. Otherwise we would have been out of the race for sure. Finally they said sleep, and I went right out.

Later we all woke up and got to talking. Nobody knew if we would be allowed to continue, so we decided we would go and do our dogs, see how that went, and check back in later. All five of us had declared the start of our mandatory twenty four hour layover, usually done upon entering a checkpoint, so we figured to spend that time recovering, tending to our teams, and lobbying for permission to continue the race.

By the time I got back into my gear and outside, my dogs were all awake. They were rolling around playing, and probably looking for me to feed them. I guess I took too long for little Jib Sheet. She had chewed herself loose from the gangline, and had raided my whitefish cache piled up by my sled. She looked up timidly at me, knowing that chewing lines really makes me mad, but cheered up when I just bent down to pet her and remove her to the team.

So, like the others, I spent the afternoon working with my dogs and napping. I felt like I had a huge hangover. Since that was nothing new, I was not really very troubled by my condition, even though we figured that twenty more minutes in that tent would have killed us. Most mushers don't count close calls. Newspaper reporters visited with us, and in the evening a TV anchorman got my story on the radiophone. By that time it had been decided that as long as we all stuck together for one or two checkpoints, we could go on. Just before my time was up, I was in the cabin sorting out my gear, and was able to watch the TV news account of our story. That was pretty neat. That was the first of three times I made the news on this race. Within 100 miles of this place, I'd be in there again.

Finally it was time to go, and I breathed a sigh of relief as I pulled the hook that held my twenty-dog team in place. Let me tell you that I breathed that sigh of relief about two hours too early. Those twenty dogs, fully rested, fully fed, fully hydrated, fully recovered from the earlier trail took my barely recovered from mostly dead self on the wildest, hardest ride I've been on since the Farewell Burn the year before. The outgoing trail goes over the backside of the checkpoint hill, around to the left, down a big hill to the right, and out into the night. Before I had gotten over the top of the hill I was dragging out of control with the sled on its side. I managed to right it in time to fall over to the other side and smash into a live spruce. The team kept on going, so I figured the tree had destroyed my sled, since we hit so quick. When we crashed to a stop at the bottom of the hill, I planted my snow hook deep and went to look at the carnage. I tell you what. That Martin, he builds a tough sled. I had a twenty foot spruce tree jammed up in my brush bow and bridle. Nothing broke except that tree. My gangline didn't break. My sled didn't break. Nothing broke. My 400-pound operation must have hit that tree at 20 mph. Amazing. So, I got my axe and chopped the tree out from in my sled, jumped back on the runners and took off again. I think the carbon monoxide was still whispering to me.

I fell over lots more times, and sweated buckets until I decided enough was enough. I had made up short chains to wrap my runners with, "rough locking" the sled and slowing the team. I had planned to use them going down the icy Dalzell Gorge this year, but stopped the sled three miles out of Finger Lake and did it up in the deep, level snow. The dogs had to huff and puff quite a bit for the next ten miles, but happily we went at a more reasonable pace. I praised the dogs often for "Going easy", and dropped down the killer stairs without incident to the Happy River. Along the way, we took a break when we drove up on a guy with a tent on the trail. He had a generator going, and his tent strung with Christmas lights. His camp was a pretty surprising sight out there in the middle of nowhere. At the bottom of the stairs, on the Happy River, I took the chains off and repacked them, then took off up the opposite cliff for a nice, pitch black twenty five more miles to Rainy Pass checkpoint.

Thanks to our early twenty four hour layover we were well behind most of the other teams by this time, so I was able to pick a spot that would shoot me out straight down the outgoing trail. The checkpoint there is on the shore of Puntilla Lake, one hundred yards from the lodge complex where we could sleep. Most of my team was no worse for the extra hard pulling I made them do. Even Whaler, who had the sore wrist, was looking good. Solo though, my boy, was limping pretty badly. During my chores I massaged his shoulders and tried to make him comfortable, but figured I'd have to drop him here.

The rest of the team was pretty frisky. The head checker there commented a couple of times on my leaders, who didn't want to sleep, but were yipping and yapping, while they clowned around with each other. That was mainly Little Foot jumping on King. I told him who the dogs were, and that they were yearling and old man. And I told him that was the best dog in the whole race. That wasn't the first time, nor the last, by a long shot that I made that brag on Little Foot. That little dog is so tough, so brave, so trusting, and such a great leader; every time I hooked her up I felt like the luckiest guy in the world. She loves to pass teams, barking at the other dogs all the way by. She'll go into open water for me, and off the trail on command. She doesn't seem to like it anywhere else but in lead, and does such a good job that I'd be a fool to let her do anything else but that.

So, as you can figure, I was pretty pleased with the team by then. They were strong, they were eating and drinking for me, and they seemed to be learning what was needed to mush on day after day. After I had taken the chains off, while they didn't seem to be worn out at all, they didn't shoot off at rocket speed. Instead they motored on at a quick, but energy-conserving, pace. The fact that they were so rambunctious at the checkpoint tended to confirm my suspicions that they could have gone faster. But instead they chose to play it smart. I thought when I started this year that I had a smooth team, and they were beginning to show me how right I was.

I did meet a nice vet there, name of Na Na (like neigh-neigh as a horse would), at least that's what her name sounded like. She would follow our group most of the race, showing up at several checkpoints down the trail. She made me laugh in the morning when I was dropping Solo. We had determined that he had developed a bruise deep in his shoulder muscles, and was in some pain. When that happens, and a dog is dropped, the first thing they like to do is give them a big shot to ease the pain and swelling. I had left him in the Dodge Lodge with Na Na to get done up and had gone back out when I started hearing him bark and scream. It sounded like they were tearing him apart piece by piece. He had made that kind of racket at the vet before the race getting his shots, so I just shook my head and laughed. Pretty soon though she came out and asked me to help hold him. I went back to the tent to find my personal, sleep-with-me pet with his mouth lashed shut with a piece of rope, and his head tied off close to a tent pole. He was dancing around, and frantically looking this way and that. Na Na called him 'sensitive'. Too 'sensitive' to inject without help. I thought it was a pretty funny situation and laughed out loud as I held him still for his shot. I was sorry to see him go, but proud of him all the same for holding up so well mentally this far into the race. He really is a sensitive creature, and had his mind blown running the Knik 200 earlier in the year. I learned when I got back to town that my good friend Kathleen, who was handling the dropped dogs in Anchorage, had Solo watching TV on a portable set, eating popcorn outside with her. He is growing to be a fantastic pet. I wasn't too sorry either to remove a dog from my team, as twenty strong Buser dogs were proving pretty tough to control.

    I also re-learned a valuable lesson at Rainy Pass this year. As I was preparing to leave in the morning, I realized that I had left my camp slippers at the lodge. I would wear them walking around while my mushing boots dried out by a fire. Anyway, the checkpoint was a long way from the lodge, so I knowingly blew off walking back to get them, like the drag last year. I really regretted leaving them when I got to the next checkpoint soaked to my waist. I decided that never again would I not go get something, or not do something I needed, just because it was inconvenient to do so at the time. Not having those shoes was a real pain several times during the race. I also left my family heirloom, vintage Baltimore Colts Zippo lighter in the outhouse there that morning, but didn't find that out 'til I was long gone. Luckily I had lots of matches.

As we were moving out of the checkpoint, a TV reporter who had just helo-ed in flagged us to a stop. He quickly asked if I had any lingering problems from the gas attack at Finger Lake, and I just as quickly told him no. Then we took off again looking like we had just left the starting line. That was twice in the news for my team. Looking back, I could argue that some of the trouble I had controlling my team out of Finger Lake could have been due to carbon monoxide effects. Nevertheless, all the mushers promised not to give any grief to Iditarod, no matter what trouble we got into. Most of us held that promise, but the one musher who was withdrawn from the race at the end of this story did not.

The mush up to the dropoff into the Dalzell Gorge was no trouble. Once again we left in the morning and drove up through a clear cold day. I remember listening to a Star Trek novel on tape during that run. That was pretty fun. On the way up I passed Lisa's team. She had left an hour or so ahead of me. We (my team) would do that a lot. We'd stay somewhere longer than the other musher, but get to the next place sooner. Martin did the same thing all through the race at the front end of the procession, and I imagine it was just as enjoyable for him. Anyway, with a little wind kicking up there on top of the world, I stopped and snacked my pooches on some tasty raw fish about a half hour from the drop into the Gorge.

Race officials had told us that the Gorge was going to be easier this year since the river ice was frozen solid. The year before, the ice was full of treacherous holes. This knowledge, plus my increasing faith in my team to be cool helped me to decide not to rough lock my sled on the way down. The descent still was a lot of work, but I never regretted that decision. The drop out of the mountains seemed to take a lot longer this year. Maybe I block out most of the first run, but I remember having to work a lot harder this year. You constantly have to be steering and braking the sled through the trees and boulders and creek beds that fill this narrow valley on the north side of the Alaska Range. So I huffed and puffed along, occasionally admonishing the dogs to " "Go easy!" ". They were right with me as I ducked and swerved down through the forest. I stopped often, and gee'd and haw'd the team a few degrees right or left to set up properly for the coming obstacle. The nineteen-dog team was still the full length, so we all were really on our toes and careful to make the descent safely. I think the dogs got reaffirmed in their trusting of the two-legs during that run. They really listened to me and worked with me as we picked our way down to ground level again. (My horse Dakota does that with me now.)

I recognized the exact tree that I smart-assedly slapped last year, losing my team in the process. The hill that that tree marks looked even longer and steeper than I remembered. I did keep my hands to myself this year, though, kept my team, and careened around the bend at the bottom with only a little pucker.

We had a few bangs, and a few bumps, but made the drop to level terrain without any major problems. The difficulty, however, was the terrain at the bottom. It was river. Most years, like last year, it is frozen over nicely. This year, there were eight inches of water flowing over the ice. I guess it is a two or three mile stretch from the base of the Dalzell Gorge to the bank where the Rohn checkpoint is, and the trail was totally under flowing water. For the first ten minutes or so, I tried to raise myself up and keep my feet dry, but since you have to keep a foot on the drag to keep the operation tight, I didn't have much luck. Pretty soon I abandoned the attempt, got back down on the submerged runners, and made Rohn twenty wet minutes or so later. My trusting dogs pulled me along with nary a hitch. That ought to be good training for Martin's race.

Rohn

Rohn Checkpoint was nice and calm, like last year. The hike to water was a little longer due to the ladder down to the river having been washed away. The food and the company were good, again like last year. After taking care of my fine dog team, I wrung out my gear, hung it up to dry, and went about fixing and repacking my sled. Like I said, I left those little shoes back in Rainy Pass, so my feet were cold and wet the whole time. I put my foot gear on last thing in the morning though, and they were mostly dry, and good to go.

At about five in the morning I got up to begin my pre-departure ablutions. Bruce and Beth Baker had already left, and Cathy was almost ready to go. These mushers were racing by their watches, which said they had been stopped long enough and it was time to leave. I, on the other hand, was waiting for daylight. I had a real, real, tough time on the trail out of Rohn last year. I made that run in the dark that time, and was not going to do that again. That's the only time in the race that I let something besides the condition of my team and my psyche determine when I would travel. I know that trail is tough, tough, tough, and wanted to do it in the daylight only. We had talked about it, those other mushers and I. I told them I was staying in the dark, and traveling in the light here. They told me they were going. So we split up for the first time since getting gassed. No sweat.

The trail was difficult from the start. On this side of Rohn, there was no open water covering the river, no snow either, just dirty glare ice, and rock bars. That lasted for a few miles, then the trail started overland, up and down hills, twisting and turning. I think a big part of my problems last year was the fact that I lost my drag brake starting that run. I had to retie mine on a few times this year, but was able to keep it on and working. Plus I had two more stashed under the sled bag, just in case I got lazy again. I think that made a big difference. Also, some mushers and fans made a few trips out to this area last summer and really cleaned up the trail. All that was left of most of the sled basher and head smacker trees were low, new stumps. They did a great job. Kudos to those guys. So I was definitely a little better in control through the Buffalo Tunnels this year.

So we were really having a good time. The dogs were working extremely well. They looked to be in good spirits, pulling up the hills and around the turns, and holding back down the declines. At one place, the trail was marked straight up the Glacier. I couldn't see any trail going around either way this time, and the dogs wanted to go straight up, so up we went. It took us a while, that maneuver, and we got snarled up in the trees along the top bank. A few dogs broke loose, but hung around like I was asking them to, and everybody was slipping and sliding on the ice. I stayed calm though, and although that situation rattled some of my dogs, we eventually made it to the trail on the other side of the creek. That was a little more than two hours into the run, and after another two or so, I crested a hill and screeched to a halt beside Cathy's team, pulled over and camped on the left side of the trail.

My team veered off to the right, into the woods such that it was going to take some axe work to get them on the trail again, so I secured the sled to a big tree, calmed my hounds, and went over to talk with broken-down Cathy. She had her sled bag opened, and all of her stuff laid out like she was at a checkpoint. I saw she was limping pretty good as we were getting our teams quiet.

She told me that she had some terrible crashes in the Buffalo Tunnels this morning, and was too injured to continue. She said that she had to drop her good leaders earlier, and her second string had whipped her around in a big U-turn as soon as they hit the glare ice out of Rohn. She said she fell off and whacked her knee badly, and had a terrible time getting to hard ground. Then she said she had trouble getting up the Glacier and smacked her knee again. Then, poor girl, she said she got cracked in the head by a low hanger, smashed off her sled, and laid out on the trail for a while. She had caught up with her team where we stood some four or five hours or so ago, and made camp. She told me that her knee was bleeding, stiff, and wrapped up too tight to move. She also said she thought she had a concussion from the tree smacker. She told me in no uncertain terms that she could not continue, and could not go back. She was waiting for rescue, and someone to drive her team out. Bummer.

I started to think of what to do with her. My team was stuck in the woods, pointed downhill, and getting more pumped up by the minute, so I couldn't really wait around, unless I wanted to make camp too. I asked Cathy if she was OK to wait for the trail sweeps and she said yes. I determined that she had dog food, fuel, and water, and decided that I'd lend her my emergency button to summon rescue. I told her, and she understood, that the emergency button was a scratch button. I told her that I would never activate it if I wanted to continue. She said rescue, and I switched it on. I hung it on her sled, told her to keep the antenna exposed, and went to chop my team out of the woods.

The rest of the run to the Farewell Lakes gradually became easier as the morning wore on.

As I found time to look around at the countryside I noticed that the hilltops and mountain crags around us were getting lower. Shortly after noon my team started skating across the small lakes which mark the end of this section of trail, and the beginning of the next.

I took it easy here and stopped to fool around with my dogs a few times. The lakes were mostly barren of snow, but every now and then I could steer the team over to an inviting patch, dump the sled over and play with my team, still nineteen dogs long. They could, if they had wanted, have pulled the sled away with little effort, but they were trained months earlier in deeper snow, when 'sled over' really meant 'team doesn't go'. Also, should they take off, I had a much better chance to grab on if the sled was low and wide, instead of tall and fast. So the dogs accepted the stops, stretched and barked at the compliments, and enjoyed the fresh, clean snow.

Presently the trees and lakes gave way to stumps and hills as we entered the Farewell Burn proper. I knew we had a really bad trail ahead of us, so I pulled over and made the dogs a quick soup with some of the last clean snow I was likely to see all afternoon. Again, they appreciated the break, did what they were told and drank, and stretched out for a while.

From the Farewell lakes there to the Kuskokwim River valley on the other side of the burn were hundreds, thousands, and hundreds of thousands of rock hard, rock shaped tussocks. They are little soil and grass knolls that freeze rock solid and are usually covered by snow. This year they weren't, and it was a four or five hour ordeal just standing on the sled. There was no trail through them. This year I passed by the turn-off to the shelter cabin I stopped at last year.

Before I had broken anything, or fallen off too many times, I passed into trees and lakes again. In short order the team dropped down through Little Nikolai, zipped up the river, went up into the big town, checked in at the check station, and parked at the school yard. The pleasant stay at Nikolai, which included a shower, some good check grub, and some good sleep, was marred only by Jill the dog showing up badly lame with a shoulder/wrist blow out. I kept her in my gangline 'til after I fed the team for the last time, then escorted her to the dog drop area. The Burn blew her up.

Also in the Nikolai check station, I was able to visit my old friend "Controversy" again when I started dealing with the Cathy situation. It seems that race officials had treated the emergency signal as a false alarm and delayed mounting formal rescue efforts despite urgings from the tracking device operators. Compounding their confusion was the fact that later mushers and motorized trail sweeps had convinced Cathy to restart her team and continue down the trail. They had turned the device off, so the tracking company didn't know what was up either anymore.

Pilots searching informally couldn't add anything useful either, so nobody did anything but fret and shake fingers over the whole affair.

After taking care of my team, I talked to my house in Big Lake on the telephone, talked to race officials at headquarters and a few others with my version of the story. Later mushers and the trail sweeps all said the same thing, so we were in the clear, but Cathy had a different story. I still don't know exactly what that was, but it wasn't like mine. I wish she had just said that she changed her mind and decided to continue. Anyway, by the time I was ready to go she hadn't shown up, so I put her to the back of my mind and headed off to McGrath, with a full belly and eighteen strong dogs. I was anxious to pick up my favorite racing sled that was waiting for me at that checkpoint, well clear of the pounding Burn.

Getting ready to go at some checkpoint. Little Foot and King still in lead.
photo: Unknown

THE MIDDLE

I was watching the dogs and the land, there on the trail to McGrath. King, Little Foot, Regatta, Orca and Jimmy Buffett made a powerful lead section. King and Jimmy Buffett kept going strong forever. Little Foot was smart as a whip, cheerful, trusting, exuberant, brave, and loved to pass other teams. Big Orca was tough as nails and pulled like a monster, and Regatta was so big he just about pulled the sled by himself. When Regatta put on the brakes to expend his used fuel, the dogs in front really had to struggle to tow him along. That was usually pretty funny.

The rest of the dogs moved around in the team regularly. I dared not keep dogs working in the wheel spot for too long at a time, so I switched both of them each time I camped. I think they appreciated that. Filling those two slots moved a lot of dogs around. Since you don't just put a particular dog in a position in the team because its previous owner moved into that dog's spot, a shuffling of teammates was constantly going on. Dogs who were stronger today maybe went further up front. Dogs that would use an easier day to regain strength gravitated to the back of the main team. I had five or six dogs whose main job was to man the wheel position. These were dogs that proved in training that they could handle the complexities of that job. They pulled the sled toward the outside of turns, away from where the rest of the team was pulling, and they were real good at not tangling their lines. Wheel dogs need a lot of room to move around, and twisted up lines hold them close to the gangline, which is going where the other dogs are pulling. They had faith that I would not run them over, and were strong enough to absorb the jerking around that the sled right behind them was constantly dishing out. The musher tries to minimize this jerking but the wheelers get the worst of any slips.

I think the team as a whole understood the way l was setting the individuals up. As individuals I think they were able to predict on some level what they would be asked to do in the future. I think it made sense to them. I know they appreciated it, whatever they thought.

We made McGrath early in the night. It was getting cold. I did my dogs, mumbling compliments on how we were doing. I retrieved the tracker that had traveled via air from Nikolai to here. As anticipated and drooled over, I got into my favorite sled. Good riddance to the twisted bent up thing I smashed out of Finger Lake with!! Hello Black Mamba!! (My black racing sled, another toboggan, but my sweetie from last year.) My checker friend let me use her sleeping space to catch some zzzzz's. My food was good and the toilet at the bar was comfortable. I also got to see Cathy withdrawn from the race and watch her stomp around steaming – make that limp around steaming. I sympathized with her anger about getting the boot, but thought she should have just quit when she said "Quit".

I had done my dog chores, slept, and moved into my perfect sled by three or four in the morning. We were ready to go. Takotna was only twenty-some miles away, and Ophir another thirty beyond that. I planned to zip thru Takotna, nice town that it is, and camp in Ophir to rest up for the fifty-mile run to Cripple (half-way point).

The checkers told me that leaving McGrath would be easy, just follow the orange tape to the right, down onto the Kuskokwim River. It didn't work that way though. It was dark, orange surveyor's tape was everywhere and we missed the turn. We drove to the end of town and had to do a 180 on the street. U-turns with a 90-foot dog team are a trick, but I had good dogs who knew to take it easy. So I rode the sled around and went back to look for the turn out of town. I missed it and wound up back at the checkpoint. "Just past the airstrip" they said. Another 180 and we drove to the end of town again. This time, at the end we took a left and drove through some residential properties on our turn around. We ended up on a sidewalk with a building on one side and a metal railing on the other. I did some tricky sled driving to snake my sled out the little break in the railing across from the building's door, and down toward the river headed for Takotna. Good dogs. They knew the program, nobody got stressed, and we looked pretty good flying up and down the street in the cold dark.

It was a nice, cold run through some low mountains to the checkpoint. To the left, on top of a tall hill is an incongruously human construction. A big, round, geodesic radar dome sits up there looking as out of place as a grapefruit on an engine block. It's fun to look at though, helps to pass the time, and lets a musher know he is on the right track.

The run to Takotna is really quite fun. It doesn't seem like a guy is going uphill very much, but the last few miles into town are downhill big time. Whoo-hooo! Yee-haaa! I mean like two or three miles down a great big ski run, complete with whoop-ti-doos, moguls, trees, and 90 degree turns. We were at it in the perfect time of day, early morning, after sleeping and feeding, and good and cold. What a blast. When we finally zipped up the bank and back down into town, the dogs were frost covered, tail wagging, and rolling in the snow, ready for more. I think if they had six-guns on them, they would be shooting in the air and waving tequila bottles like a bunch of vaqueros at fiesta time. I however, choked back the impulse to un-holster my Ruger stainless six-shooter .357.

Last year in Takotna I spent more time than I wanted… eating. This is a great village and they go all out for the Iditarod. This year I stuck to my plan and only snacked the dogs, changed their booties, and accepted a sack lunch from the townspeople. We were on the road in forty-four minutes. Near a record for me.

It was a pretty long haul around to Ophir. First we go up and up along one side of the mountain range. We are on a road. The road slants to the side for drainage, creating a long winding side hill. Normally that condition spawns much cursing and sweating. We have to work hard to keep the sled going straight on a side hill. It's hard on the dogs too. We lean way out, pull the sled over on one runner and try and balance it there so we don't slip down the grade, or climb up the other side. We are constantly heaving on the handle bow, alternately dragging foot for balance or hopping around trying not to tip over. I think wind surfers look the same way. They seem to be always pulling and flapping the sail around, even when they go straight. It looks like a lot of work. I imagine though that it is a lot of fun. Like this particular piece of trail. I guess the fact that it is all in one direction, up, and all smooth, makes it easier than the standard side hill situation. Anyway, it was fun there having fried chicken and Pepsi while tipping around on one runner.

Then we went down and around the other side of the hill through old mining camps strewn with rusting pieces of huge earth moving equipment. My team powered up the incline handsomely, but began to slow on the way down. I let them take it easy and twiddled my thumbs as we wound down the hill side. Most of the structures there were little more than plywood shacks, all falling down, but I could see where the top bananas of the operation would stay. There were some nice two-story, regulation houses every other mile or so.

I don't remember too much about the long stay in Ophir. I know I spent some time massaging and evaluating Endeavor's wrists and ankles. He is a big cross-eyed machine, and a fine asset to the team. I had to drop him though. Most of the trail from here to Nome is pretty easy, dog speaking, but there were six-hundred miles to go. Poor guy, last thing I did before booting up and going the next evening was to lead that fine worker over to the drop dog stake-out and rub him down one last time. He recovered OK right quick after the race… and got sold.

About the only other thing I remember, besides the beautiful vet on station there, is spending a lot of time playing with my team. The checkers and vets seemed to get a kick out of watching; somebody even was taking some pictures, so I got kind of egged on and spent quite some time, on several occasions, on my back in the snow with my pals. Also, I didn't see any of the other mushers who had pulled up doing much of that, and I could see how much happier my dogs looked. So that was a good deal. Then I dropped Endeavor, booted up, popped the hook, passed the left hand turn, went down the wrong trail, and wound up on an airfield. "Screech!!!" U-ee. Down the same trail, right at the turn, and off through the night to Cripple, the halfway point on the Innoko River. Mushers figure distance to there by how many river crossings they make.

Cripple

The team flew down the trail. It is a little over fifty miles between those checkpoints. The checkers at Cripple didn't expect me for seven hours or so, and after five and a quarter we set the hook around midnight in a checkpoint asleep. The team really surprised me. They didn't want to stop along the way. Twice, at river crossings, I stopped and tried to snack them, but nobody ate, nobody made noise; they just stood there waiting to go again. It sure sent me to scratching my head. My first year Ophir to Iditarod (southern route half-way point) was a crawl. No fun. This year was the opposite. We were zipping along through the woods with the blowing snow at our backs and nothing but black forest around us for scores of miles in any direction.

Suddenly out of the darkness, two big eyes sped over the front of my dog team from left to right. A moose had crossed the trail on the move within feet of my team. It must have turned to look at us on the way as I clearly saw two eyes about six feet off the ground. In an instant we were past the spot, with only the adrenaline rush remaining.

The checkpoint was asleep. I secured my team, bedded the dogs down and went off in search of my drop bags. I had been a checker there three years ago and had to haul every one of every musher's seventy-pound drop bags up the bank from the river to the checkpoint. The supply aircraft land on the river, and the dog teams park up on the bank. So after searching the compound to no avail, I reluctantly headed down to the river to find the bags lined out where they had landed with the plane. There was a wonderful set up for the media, with sidewalks, tents, signs, even an outhouse made out of carved and stacked snow blocks, but little in the way of creature comforts for the mushers.

The checkers were nice guys from this area though, and we had a fine time. The communications tent turned out to be where everybody hung out. We gossiped, drank lots of coffee, and made some home video while I wound down and fixed some gear. I had fed my dogs hours ago, so I went out to make them some more, and fed that out, before I went to sleep around eight in the morning.

I woke around four or five in the afternoon and performed my ablutions as the sun was sinking, taking the thermometer mercury with it. Leaving Cripple here around midnight was where the race really got tough for me. Half way in.

Cripple to Ruby, 120 miles, minus forty-five Fahrenheit, midnight. That was a pretty tough run. When it's that cold, a guy can't uncover to eat, drink, smoke, spit, anything. All I could do was shuffle my chemical hand warmers around in my mittens and try to stay on the sled. The bitter cold had frozen my boot soles and sled-runner foot pads so hard that there was no friction between them. Frozen bumpy plastic on frozen bumpy plastic. As the trail wound through creek beds and gullies I was forever slipping off and banging my elbows and knees hanging on to the moving sled. Each time I flailed around on back of the sled, I'd open up a new place for the cold to zip into my suit and laser cut through me to the bone.

The dogs, however, were doing fine. They all had their coats and booties on, and were comfortable in the cold. There was not much wind, the night was clear, and the trail was good. I think they enjoyed listening to the Auroras that night, as the sky was in fine form. (I didn't look around too much for freezing my face and neck.) So they motored along, without a care, for six or seven hours (with a few two-minute breaks every now and then), until the sun came back up and let some mercury back into the thermometer.

As soon as the sun cleared the hills we were mushing up and it touched my face, I pulled the team over, unhooked the tuglines, and soaked it up for a while. This was where I was making my camp for a few hours. Two thirds of the way to Ruby, first checkpoint on the Yukon River. Bless the sun!

I think Bruce was there before me, or maybe I before him, but the two of us, and later Hero Jamie and Lisa made a little fire and traded stories and food 'til we got the itch to move. As we were ready, we booted up, cleaned up, hooked up and went. Now we were mushing through the summer-time mining community of Poorman. Lots of low buildings and interesting equipment, a lot like the trail into Ophir. Alternately, Bruce and I would lose and regain sight of each other as we sped around some low mountains, always heading north to the Yukon. One neat sight, way out there in the middle of nowhere, is a huge metal bridge spanning a deep valley. It's pretty big, maybe a quarter mile long, and 200 feet or so down, so that was pretty fun to mush across. The dogs looked at it, knew it was different, but went right across.

By then it was early afternoon, and we mushed steadily up the twisty turning actual road to Ruby. The dogs made good time, and I napped and twiddled my thumbs dragging along with the sled. Bruce and I played tag some more as the sun began to set.

By and by we came to a place where there was no more uphill, and we started the descent into Ruby. I guess it is three or four miles down into the town, down a pretty good grade. I stood on the drag for the ride down, dogs loping and snow flying. We dodged a few cars and trucks as the lights of the village came up to meet us. Quick enough we swooped back up and to the right into town, then another quick two lefts into some old straw, and I set the hook. Ruby, some eighteen hours after leaving Cripple. Now all I had to do was pass on down 200 miles of Yukon River, 90 miles over to Unalakleet, then zip on up the coast, and wake up in Nome.

Ruby is a nice place, and after I cleaned up the old straw and laid out some new, cleaned up the dogs and laid out some food, I went inside the community center for some food and sleep. They had mattresses laid out in a quiet corner, and it was very comfortable.

While working with my dogs, Jamie came in and went to work on her Malamute crew. Her show dogs had terrible sores on their feet. Their feet looked great in the show ring, but had been bred away from characteristics necessary for long distance running. Their pads rubbed together with each step, and gradually became raw and painful. Vets said she had done an excellent job maintaining them, as good as humanly possible, but they were still getting worse. She would turn back in the morning, two miles out of Ruby and scratch her team.

I dropped another one of my team dogs before I left. Cortez, a thin, blond trotter, was out of gas. He wouldn't eat, wouldn't drink, and looked run down and tired. He has a funny gait that looks like it cost him a lot to maintain. He had worked his heart out to make it to the Yukon, and I sent him home with congratulations. He was later sold to a recreational musher.

The run down the Yukon was cold. It was cold at night, and it was cold during the day. Ten to thirty below, with a head wind the whole way. For the dogs, it was fabulous running. At night they had their coats on, and they all wore their booties, and so were very comfortable. They ran fast. We still left checkpoints late and passed teams, and I remember passing two mushers around a big rock island like they were standing still. Little Foot the leader was especially happy during this time. She would bark at teams as we went by, and bark at the air for reasons of her own. She was a joy to watch.

Ruby, Galena, Nulato, Kaltag, we flew. Our times through there were our fastest ever. The dogs had a great time. Of course, we still took the scenic routes out of town. In Nulato especially, since the checkpoint was high above town, as far away from the river as we could get. Most of the race had passed here long ago, so the trail stakes marking the way through town were virtually gone. If we had gone the planned way, we would have gone down onto the river via the snow ramp, and had no trouble. As it was, we weren't even close by the time we had descended through town, and crashed down the bank onto the river.

During that thrashing around, my personal food cooler had flown out of my sled bag, still attached by its lanyard, and been crushed under my sled one time when it fell over. The lid had come off, so I had to turn the team back up the riverbank, over to our trail again, and halfway down, where I could pick up my wayward equipment. I was not going to leave gear behind anymore. Only then could we settle down to some serious flat land, cold weather mushing.

The only low point, besides the cold, was when I had to leave Lafite, the excellent team dog, in Nulato. Her shoulders had given out, and she could not continue. She went on to finish Iditarod XXIII in '95 in Martin's second place team.

Kaltag

So, just around sunrise, fifteen dogs strong, we piled into Kaltag, ready to rest up and make for the coast. I didn't stay long, less than eight hours, and didn't sleep at all. I worked on my dog team, worked on my gear, ate a bunch of food, and watched my dogs rest. As soon as they began to stir, I got ready to go. I tried to get Lisa to head out with me, but she had to sleep more.

I'll spend a little time on this episode as it cost her the race. Her team was a little slower than those of the mushers she was traveling with: me, Bruce, and Beth (Jamie and the Malamutes were even slower). Consequently, Lisa was always having to play catch-up. She would get into a checkpoint after us, and try to leave a little before. So, her dogs got a little less rest than ours at any point. However, while we were staying fourteen to sixteen hours, that wasn't much of a problem.

In Kaltag, however, she left way behind us. Also, at at least one of the two shelter cabins on the way to Unalakleet, she took a six to eight hour break. All of us took some down time on that run (Bruce and Beth at Tripod Flats, and me at Old Woman), but she got even further back. We took regular long rests in Unalakleet, and as she was heading in as we headed out, she cut her team's rest even further so we wouldn't get beyond Shaktoolik without her. Turns out that she was about halfway through her rest when we all left Shaktoolik, so she ran out, and caught us seven or eight hours into Koyuk. By then her dogs were done.

We spent our regular long time in Koyuk, and saw a very tired Lisa appear as we were bedding down ourselves. When everybody left in the morning, her dogs wouldn't go. They had to rest. As we traveled on, we heard that she tried several times through the afternoon and night to get them to move, but it was a no go. She scratched in Kaltag and flew her team home to Nome. Tough break, but they are animals, not machines.

So, back to the race trail. Kaltag was behind me, and one of my favorite trails was under the runners. The dogs were cooking. They had built up some reserve flying down the Yukon with such long breaks, and they flew out of Kaltag into the Western sun. The trail outbound from Kaltag winds around through woods and swamps, and is pretty easy to follow. The wind was picking up though, and I knew it would be blowing further on down in the flats. Sure enough, we came into some open spots that precede the real Flats, and the wind was a blowing. From the north, fifteen to twenty knots and kicking up snow. I knew it could have been miserable and was crushed at the thought of my team's fine spirits turning to depression. So, I played some mind games with my dogs and had a great time.

I made like mushing through the wind was the greatest thing in the world. As we passed out of cover and into the wind, I would hoot and holler at the dogs, calling them by name, praising them, the wind, the race, the snow, everything. Again, we flew. The dogs got so pumped up that they would race out of momentary shelter and into the blowing snow. Little Foot again was barking at trees. I felt great, and the team had a blast.

Kaltag to Unalakleet is a long way. Truly ninety miles. Shelter cabins divide the run roughly in thirds. As I came on the first Tripod Flats cabin on a little creek, Bruce and Beth were just leaving. They were just getting their dogs going, and since we had a full head of steam on, Zoom, we passed them on the fly and left them in the dust. The dogs looked so good I didn't dare stop them. They had settled down to steady pulling and we made the next thirty miles or so to Old Woman cabin in fine style. That shelter cabin is in the woods, on a running creek. While I stopped there to feed dogs and change booties, Bruce and Beth went on by. Little less than four hours later I was off.

Earlier in the race, some young rookies had camped out here and been scared by wolves. They were camped at night, and say they were surrounded by glowing eyes. Their dogs were spooked, suddenly barking and whining, and the men were scared. They didn't want to shoot, for fear of being overrun. I guess they had a wild time there, but I didn't hear of it 'til after the race, and the wolves didn't visit my team.

So, I lit out headed for Unalakleet about ten at night. Parts of that trail are really fun. Acres and acres are thickly wooded, and the trail cuts a winding path through. It is fun to mush a trail like that, steering around curves and ducking low hanging branches. The dogs were still in good spirits, and we made good speed.

All too soon the fun stuff was over, and we headed toward the beach. The woods disappeared, and as we mushed up onto flat land again, I passed Beth headed into the featureless dark. Almost featureless, that is. There is a red light on top of a radio tower out there that drove me crazy. Since I could see it from such a long way off, it took a long time to reach it. All the time I was thinking it was Unalakleet. It is, though, just a radio tower out in the middle of nowhere. When we passed it and there was no town, I got a little frustrated. About the time we passed that light though, more lights hove into view. We dropped down onto a river slough and headed for them and I figured it must be Unalakleet. No such luck. It is some kind of industrial park out there.

So on we mushed to the third lights, finally Unalakleet. We followed the markers off the cold slough, over on to the beach, and up into town. The dogs still looked strong after running eight of the last twelve hours. I was ready for a nap, though, and after caring for my team for a few hours, hit the sack. Mushers sleep upstairs in the gymnasium and I fell to sleep to the sound of basketball playing. It lulled me right out.

Camping out.
photo: Martin Buser

THE END

Unalakleet is a nice place. Larger cargo planes can land there, so the town is built up pretty well. Mushers can pick from several eating establishments and shop at a well stocked store. I did both, having two hamburgers and some new sunglasses. Sometime around noon, it was time to move again.

The dogs were eager, the team still fifteen strong, and we burnt up the rolling tundra, heading to the base of the Blueberry Hills. That's a pretty steep and long climb up and over the headlands where a line of hills meet the sea. The wind was blowing again, and it was cold again, so it was work getting to the top. The trail follows creeks and gullies, searching out a continuous climb to the tippy top. Crossing the Alaska Range, the trail crests between two peaks. Crossing the Blueberry Hills, the trail crests right over the top of the tallest hill.

Then it's down, down, down. It is pretty steep, and it follows the same kinds of contours that the uphill side does. That makes for some exciting mushing. This time, the north wind was still blowing, only now it was blowing uphill. So I was fumbling with my goggles, which kept fogging up, fighting to slow and steer the sled, which kept wanting to tip over, and trying to duck the wind at the same time, which wanted to rip my face off. It was great! I really had a good time going down this year.

Exhausted and still excited, we landed on the beach again, and stopped to snack. A snowmachiner came down after us, and we spent a little time talking about I don't know what. Pretty soon, with the dogs threatening to yank the snow hook out, we ran down onto the ice headed for Shaktoolik, on the Norton Sound. It was dark by then, and

Shaktoolik's lights were bright. I knew this to be a short run, so the lights at night didn't bother me. Sure enough, they quickly got brighter and clearer. Some years they have fierce storms there, but this time it was calm and cool.

Nighttime temperatures had warmed up to a balmy twenty below, so I was comfortable doing my chores, and spent a lot of time fooling around with the dogs. Each foot got the ice picked out of it. Each foot got salve massaged in between the toes. Little Foot, Orca, and a few others who had been running with sore wrists got some different salve massaged in. Big Chester had a sore shoulder, and he got a massage and a heat pack taped under his doggie blanket. Each dog got straw packed around him after he settled down, and each got a good night kiss. This was pretty much the routine during the whole race, but having it comfortably warm outside made it much nicer for us all.

We left for Koyuk with the rising sun. After heading out in the wrong direction, getting corrected, and passing the Mile 18 Island, I went to sleep. I was sitting on my sled seat watching the dogs run, getting tireder and tireder. The team was moving like one big animal, each part swaying in rhythm to all the others. Colorful blankets on the smaller dogs focused attention on their movements until I would lose myself in that undulating patch of green on the stark white ice. I'd snap out of that trance and get stuck watching the dogs' feet. All the colorful booties weaving in and out in perfect time were too much. I imagined that I could feel the slight tug that each footfall gave the gliding sled.

I knew I was going under, and I knew the dogs would take care of me. They were moving in such perfect harmony; as long as I was there, everything was perfect for them, and they didn't need anything else from me. It was with a smile on my face that I tied a line around my back and put my head down. Four hours later, I opened my eyes 200 yards out of Koyuk.

I spent the rest of the afternoon caring for and rolling around with my dog team. Over the protests of race officials up the line, I slept a full night there, BS'ing with Bruce, Beth, the trail sweeps, and the checkers. Lisa pulled in late, but she was busy and tired. I guess the big topic of conversation was Bruce's marriage proposal that he had videotaped and sent on ahead up the trail to Diana Dronenburg. She accepted, and I think sent the video of that moment back down to him.

So, where are we? Koyuk to Elim; half a day's run along the coastline, west. That is another nice mush if we stay out of storms. The weather was good for my team and me, and we traveled alone. I forget who left when, but I don't think I saw any others 'til White Mountain. The trail is on the sea ice, following the coastline. We travel sheltered from the north wind in the shadow of huge rock cliffs and bluffs. Geological history is written with broad strokes by the tilted strata to the team's right.

Twice on the way to Elim we drove through camps abandoned in winter. The first, we traveled right through. It seemed to be on a little island, close inshore. It is full of wooden houses and three-sided shacks. Fish and gear drying racks make a slalom course we mushed through. Not a soul was there, though. No footprints, only speeding snowmachine tracks, and of course the occasional dog turd.

The second was a line of shacks pointing out to sea, with some big antenna providing contrast. Then, as the race course does some years, we followed the trail off the water and up a big headland. This is close to Elim. We picked up a road on the top of the rock, and mushed on for another half hour to end up on the back side of the village. I didn't spend long in Elim this year. Four hours was all I needed to soup and feed the team, gobble some grub myself, change booties and go. The young girls there wanted me to stay, but this was the coast, and I was determined to make it into Nome as fast as my dog team could get me there. So, the dogs had a little nap in the sun, and we were off.

Elim to White Mountain, actually Elim to Golovin, is half sea ice, and half mountain. The sea part is more of the trail inbound to Elim. Pretty nice. The overland part is up Little McKinley Mountain. Pretty tall.

My first year, the dogs had a big rest in Elim and ran up the mountain like it wasn't there. This year we didn't take that long rest, and it was a different story.

We ran along the sea ice as the sun set, and started up the Walla Walla Hills as darkness was coming on. These seem to be the foothills of the range that has Little McKinley as its highest seaward point. The trail goes up and down, in and out of gullies and little patches of trees. The dogs were going well, and had settled in and were pulling strong... up, down, and around. There is a shelter cabin there for when the wind blows, but we passed it by.

Presently the trail curved up again, this time with no down. Just up. We carved wide curves as we headed back and forth up the mountainside. From about half way up, the dog team began to slow down. I was hoping we could make it to the top. I knew it was not far, but sure enough one team dog sat down and stopped the whole team. I got out and rubbed her down and stood her back up and got the team moving, but then one of her sisters put her butt on the snow and the team stopped again. The other dogs looked back at me as if to say "What's going on?" I didn't have an answer.

I went through this routine a few more times, with up to three dogs stopping the team, and realized I had a real problem. So, without getting too upset, I took a piece of line up to the front, petting heads along the way and telling them to get ready. I became the lead dog there, climbing up the hill. My dog team followed me, and if anyone sat down, the rest of the dogs took their cue from me, and kept pulling. Once or twice, I slipped my rope out of the line, and tried to wave the team on by. No go. They all stopped and looked at me as if to say "Forget it bud, get out and pull." Half an hour or so later, we got on top, and I got back on the runners.

The Little McKinley adventure was not over yet though. The wind had picked up a little, scouring the mountain top clean and wiping out the trail. I don't know why, but the dogs lost the scent, and we drifted off the ridge to the right until we started sliding down the wrong side. I yelled for the dogs to go haw, back up the side, but that didn't work and we kept going down.

The snow was hard packed, and my foot brake wouldn't bite. I only swung the team around so we were headed straight down. I dumped the sled over to try and stop, but by that time we had built up a pretty good head of steam and nothing was going to stop us but level ground. Snow was flying and cracking, the dogs were yipping and yapping, I was yelling, and the sled was scraping the hillside as we rocketed down. It must have been quite a spectacle, and surely was an exciting ride. There was a snowmachiner up on the trail. Maybe he saw.

I figure we went eight hundred feet or so off the trail and two or three hundred feet down.

We had landed on a lower terrace covered with scrub trees and rock outcroppings. I looked the team over after the wild ride down and they were panting from the run, but no one had gotten tangled or dragged, and they lined out looking to go again. I had a general sense of where the trail was, and the dogs pointed themselves in that direction. We had to twist and wind our way through the bushes and rocks, outright climbing as much as mushing.

At first, the dogs were hesitant about pushing through the thin spots in the brush like I needed them to in order to cut a line up to the trail. I encouraged and praised them from the front of the team as I led the leaders. Soon they became happy again. As their old confidence in me came back, I was able to direct the team from the runners. An hour later, by the time we regained the trail, we were all happy and the dog team was smoking down the trail, again toward sea level, and Golovin.

That takes another hour and a half or so, and I became very tired. It was one or two in the morning, clear and cold. My team was running well, and I climbed onto my sled bag, head first, and dozed. Soon enough we came into the Golovin checkpoint. I stopped the sled, and snacked the dogs while waiting for the checker to bundle up and come out. I can't remember if it was a he or a she, but shortly after my gear was checked, we waved good by, and I was off for White Mountain. I only remember the last part, a cold, dark mush up a frozen river. The checker, an old native, was out with his headlight, and I aimed the team for him. He checked if we needed a vet immediately, "No", and brought us our stuff, water and straw included. Room service is nice.

While I was doing the camp chores, as they always did, the vet came out. The last two vets had been traveling up the trail with the last group since Unalakleet. The woman called Na Na and an English sounding man named Doug. Fine and cheery spirited folks, they told me which dogs to massage, and where. They changed out the wraps on the wrists and pasterns that they had put on in the last checkpoint. They were especially great about that. They'd change the wrap when we got in, and just before we left.

They had personally monitored the team since Shaktoolik and Unalakleet, and so were savvy on the condition of each dog. The dogs they worked on regularly knew them and accepted their ministrations indifferently. The veterinary corps learns on the job on Iditarod. These two were fast becoming experts on how to keep dogs working healthy, when lack of very particular care would scratch them. I hadn't dropped a dog since the Yukon River, and Iditarod veterinarians can take a lot of the credit for that.

White Mountain

From White Mountain, fifty-five miles to Safety, and another twenty-two to the Finish Line. We left White Mountain checkpoint early after sun-up with the sled as light as I could make it. Like the first year, since Koyuk I had been shipping stuff home. I no longer had much of a 'personal bag'. Gone were the extra sets of batteries and redundant head lamp systems. The frying pan, blank book, half-a-dozen music tapes, half-a-score brass snaps, all went home. Pounds of hoarded foot medicine, wrist wraps, back-up harnesses, the second cooler, dozens of booties… Outa here! The gang line was de-forested and the accumulated snow and ice was knocked off the sled.

So set, the dogs and I set out for the Topkok Hills. Bruce was almost in Nome, and Beth was an hour or so ahead of me. The team powered up and down the ridges of the last set of hills as the sun rode its peak overhead. On the westernmost side of the range I could see the beach stretching off into the mist. I could see the shelter cabin at the base of the hills where I rested the year before and wrote Tatters' name on the wall. Beyond that I couldn't really make anything out as the ground appeared to be covered by mist. The sky was clear though.

My team caught up with Beth's at the cabin. As we chatted about the freshening breeze and the run over Topkok, the trail sweeps drove up and told us we had better get a move on. A storm was going on now, and was likely to get worse before getting better. They promised to stay on the marked trail on their way into Safety, and told us to keep them in sight.

So we took their advice and headed out. As soon as we left the vicinity of the cabin and dropped down onto a frozen lagoon the wind hit. It was coming from our right, and immediately blew the sled around 90 degrees from our direction of travel. That was a pretty tough half-mile with the dogs turned sideways in their traces, pulling into the wind and moving sideways to it. We got off the ice then and headed out into the strong middle of the storm.

Ground storms are strange phenomena to travel through. A musher can be struggling through wind blown hell, with his gear flapping in the gale and the snow sandblasting his face, and look up and see clear skies and airplanes flying. The storm layer is only a hundred feet thick, with a very different weather pattern above. Mountains to the north funnel wind down the Solomon River drainages and out to sea here. That topographical system makes up what people call the Solomon Blowhole. It is famous for moderate to severe winds and blowing snow that can last for days at a time. It was turned on today.

We kept struggling on, catching a reassuring glimpse of the trail sweeps every marker or two. Time went away, and all that was left was the fight crab-wise into the wind. The dogs were having a tough time with every shred of exposed fur (coats on) thoroughly frosted and sculpted to windward. King and Little Foot put their shoulders into the wind and drove the team westward. They must have been able to sense the trail, or hear the snowmachines or something. I was in a whiteout from one marker to the next. Visibility was about two dog teams in any direction but upwind, where it was almost nothing.

We can only be so tough for so long. Sure enough, as I feared, the team broke and turned hard out to sea. I knew if I lost the trail here, we were goners. There are no markers on the sea ice. There are large open leads. So I threw the sled over on its side and sat on it to stop the team. As soon as we stopped, the dogs wound up into a shivering, whining huddle.

I also knew that if we really stopped moving here, we were sunk too. I had to get the team straightened out and moving again. I think the dogs just took a little break, because there was not much trouble from them to line us out again. I reassured each of them as best as I could, brushing the worst of the frost off their faces and shaping up their coats. I had to undo a few snaps to untangle the huddle the dogs made, and it felt like I was grabbing hot iron as I worked the snaps. My polypro gloves saved me some real trouble, but just the same I frostbit the tips of all my right hand fingers. They hurt all the way to Nome.

I got the team pointed toward Nome again and jogged with the leaders for a few paces before I jumped on again. Beth and I had been leapfrogging each other and I caught up with her again. Just as I passed her and thought her dogs would follow, they broke for the sea. The last I saw of her on the race trail, she was grinding her foot brake against the frozen tundra, her big parka back catching the wind and pushing her south to Unalakleet.

Rescue teams found her five miles from Safety, a mile or so out to sea. She had finally stopped and bedded her team down the best she could, and crawled into her sled bag for protection from the relentless wind. I'm sure she looked up and saw the clear sky darkening with oncoming night.

She mushed her team to Safety the next afternoon, but scratched there with badly frostbitten hands, and tired and hungry dogs.

So there was my competition for the last-place Red Lantern, blown out by the storm. All I had to do was make it into Nome.

Not long after Beth's team took a dive, the road to Safety appeared, and the wind started to stack off. We were entering the far edge of the storm, and the road provided a good trail. As night came on, the mile markers ticked down to twenty-two, and the Safety roadhouse hove into view.

I spent somewhere close to an hour there. I stripped off the dogs' booties and fed them everything left in the sled, then went in for some warmth myself. I got some coffee, juice, and a hot sandwich, and went over Beth's situation with the checkers and trail sweeps. They would mount a search at first light, and I would go on to Nome.

The team was willing, and I was anxious as we set out on the last two and a half hours of *Iditarod Two* for me, and *Iditarod One* for my team. The trip was mostly uneventful. Up and over the cape, and toward the lights of Nome.

Nome

My first year I lost the trail here and headed into town from the back side. This time I lost it and stayed on the road on the seaward side. The asphalt was blown clear, so my sled runners quickly scraped down to wood and metal, but I didn't care. A couple of times the team wanted to take me off to the right, where they knew the trail was, but I didn't want any of that. We were on the same road the Finish Line was on, and we weren't getting off.

I heard the siren when I reached the outskirts of town, and picked up the police escort soon after as the team ran along the snow covered sidewalk down Front Street. Just before the finishing chute I got in front of the leaders to guide them under the Burled Arch that marks the end of the race.

Friends helped me take the booties off the grateful dogs, who knew something different was in the air. They rolled around a little bit and rubbed up against each other as I congratulated them. Someone handed me a beer and a small crowd spent a little time petting the dogs and talking with me.

The race Marshall checked my gear and declared me an official finisher at sixteen days, sixteen hours, seventeen minutes, thirty five seconds. The fastest Iditarod Red Lantern time. We took the team to wonderful hosts Pat and Sue's house and laid them down in houses filled with fresh straw. King, Little Foot, Orca, Jimmy Buffett finished in the lead section. Regatta, Racket, Chester, Tom, and Jamie pulled strong in the front of the team. Dolphin, Beluga, Jib Sheet, Barracuda, Pirate, and Whaler, the 'floaters', rounded out the rest of the team. Finito.

You learn to look around more. You find yourself during, and after, the race looking around, up, over your shoulder. It becomes important to know what where you are looks like, and what it looks like in relation to where you were the last time you looked. Also, it's good not to take the beauty of your surroundings for granted.

With Solo the pet dog. RIP Solo 1999.
photo: Kathy Chapoton

At the Late Finisher's banquet; miming driving the sled.
photo: Unknown

Again.
photo: Kathy Chapoton

EPILOGUE

Before I finished the note describing the 1994 Iditarod (in April 1995), the 1995 Iditarod had come and gone. Martin finished a tough second to Doug Swingly, and earned the Leonhard Seppala Humanitarian Award for outstanding care of his dogs. Our yearling driver this year finished thirty-something-th with ten tough little dogs. My friend Tim Triumph was disqualified for failing to meet a time deadline to Unalakleet, but pushed on to mush into Nome ahead of the last two official mushers. Another friend, Andy Sterns, got shut down by a storm and scratched three miles from Nome. It's a tough race.

In 1995, I did not run in the race, but vacationed in Nome at the end of Iditarod. I had a wild adventure on a snowmachine, and for your patience on this tale, I'll include that story.

Our host's house is right across Front Street from Iditarod Headquarters in Nome, so I spent quite a little time there. One morning, I picked up the job of riding a snowmachine and towing a sled out to Safety to pick up a volunteer and two dropped dogs. I had already ridden out once to get one of Martin's dogs, so I thought it would be easy money. There were a number of things I should have watched out for, but didn't, making the trip more eventful than it should have been.

So I headed out of town into the growing breeze. (Watch-out: Ignorant of the weather.) (Watch-out: Snowmachine cross-country alone.) Halfway to the base station, the trailer hitch broke off the machine, and I had to rig it back up with bungee cords.

The wind was blowing pretty good, but for a while I still had the trail.

Along about mile eight or so, I started losing the trail, getting blown out to sea for some yards before turning back inland and lucking into a trail marker. Over and over, I'd try to drive straight, but wind up off the beach, and on the ice (the ground looks different). Finally I missed the trail all together and zoomed up the hillside of Cape Nome. The trail was on the seaward side of the cape, but I had missed it on my last recovery inland.

I thought, well no problem. I'll just go over the top and catch the trail on the other side. (Watch-out: Going over a hill when the other side is unknown.) I guess I drifted seaward again, and soon found myself sliding down an ever steeper hill side. I thought I'd just bottom out soon and be OK, but the only thing that would come out of the blowing snow toward me was more hill. By this time I was out of control and in short order the machine flipped, throwing me off. I landed in a ball in the snow as the machine and sled rolled over me and headed on down. I stopped in time to see it crash into some alders sticking out of the snow. Amazingly the sled was still attached.

I slid down and pulled the machine out of the trees. Looking down, that's all there was – down. I could see clumps of more alders, so I took off aiming for the nearest. I figured to crash into successive alder bunches to slow my decent. Two or three times that worked pretty well. I'd take off in the right direction, lose control on the way down, and fetch up in a tangle of alders to aim again anew.

At last I could see a line of black, and figured that was the ground. About half way down, I realized that it was a cliff edge and bailed off my careening machine. I stopped on my butt and watched the big green trail machine, then the big silver sled, disappear over the edge. I saw a puff of snow a little later that suggested that my transport had come to a rest.

Turns out the drop off was not vertical, and the distance to ground was less than twenty feet. The machine had landed flat on its tread with the motor still running. The sled was another story though. It had flipped over and inside out in its bridle, smashing flat the snow machine back seat rest and scattering its contents out on the road.

That was exciting. I straightened everything out, picked up the broken off pieces, and headed off again toward Safety (what a good name for that place). Soon enough though, in the storm again I got lost. Again and again, blown out to sea, zip back up onto the land. Finally I reached buildings that mark the way to the roadhouse. But when I turned around to look, my trailer sled was gone!

I doubled back a few times until I lost sight of the houses, but couldn't see any sled and decided to flunk myself and get to Safety. Once there, I told my story to the volunteers, and then called the race officials who sent me out there. They were happy I was alright. Except for a new limp and a fresh bruise.

Another snowmachiner who helped the race and knew the area offered to load my load on his snowmachine sled and lead us (me and the volunteer, Drop Dog Barbara) back to Nome. The only excitement there was when Barbara's goggles fogged up on the back of my machine. She got to swaying around back there, effectively blinded, until she got motion sickness. Thankfully she patted my shoulder to stop before it was too late.

Pat-the-host told me about all the things I should have watched out for. He and I went out the next day in clear weather and quickly found the lost sled.

Dog chores at Pat and Sue's in Nome.
photo: Unknown

Now, with Dakota the Horse and Hazard the Lab.
photo: Lynda Plettner

At work off the west coast of Africa these days.
photo: Jason Manina

Always though the Iditarod is something that never should escape memory. It is a break from life as sure as a trip to the moon would be. Hardly any one else has done it, and it is very different in all respects from regular life on earth. Fewer folks have finished the Iditarod than have climbed Mt. Everest. We keep photos, sled parts, dog names in memorial, and most fortunately for those who write, stories of that magical time off somewhere else.